Thomas Hart

Theodore Roosevelt

Alpha Editions

This edition published in 2023

ISBN : 9789357949453

Design and Setting By
Alpha Editions
www.alphaedis.com
Email - info@alphaedis.com

Contents

CHAPTER I.

THE YOUNG WEST.

Even before the end of the Revolutionary War the movement had begun which was to change in form a straggling chain of sea-board republics into a mighty continental nation, the great bulk of whose people would live to the westward of the Appalachian Mountains. The hardy and restless backwoodsmen, dwelling along the eastern slopes of the Alleghanies, were already crossing the mountain-crests and hewing their way into the vast, sombre forests of the Mississippi basin; and for the first time English-speaking communities were growing up along waters whose outlet was into the Gulf of Mexico and not into the Atlantic Ocean. Among these communities Kentucky and Tennessee were the earliest to form themselves into states; and around them, as a nucleus, other states of the woodland and the prairie were rapidly developed, until, by the close of the second decade in the present century, the region between the Great Lakes and the Gulf was almost solidly filled in, and finally, in 1820, by the admission of Missouri, the Union held within its borders a political body whose whole territory lay to the west of the Mississippi.

All the men who founded these states were of much the same type; they were rough frontiersmen, of strong will and adventurous temper, accustomed to the hard, barren, and yet strangely fascinating life of those who dwell as pioneers in the wilderness. Moreover, they were nearly all of the same blood. The people of New York and New England were as yet filling out their own territory; it was not till many years afterwards that their stock became the predominant one in the northwestern country. Most of the men who founded the new states north of the Ohio came originally from the old states south of the Potomac; Virginia and North Carolina were the first of the original thirteen to thrust forth their children in masses, that they might shift for themselves in the then untrodden West.

But though these early Western pioneers were for the most part of Southern stock, they were by no means of the same stamp as the men who then and thereafter formed the ruling caste in the old slave-holding states. They were the mountaineers, the men of the foot-hills and uplands, who lived in what were called the backwater counties. Many of them were themselves of northern origin. In striking contrast to the somewhat sluggish and peaceful elements going to make up the rest of its heterogeneous population, Pennsylvania also originally held within its boundaries many members of that most fiery and restless race, the Scotch-Irish. These naturally drew towards the wilder, western parts of the state, settling along the slopes of the numerous inland mountain ridges running parallel to the Atlantic coast; and from thence they drifted southward through the long valleys, until they met and mingled with their kinsfolk of Virginia and the Carolinas, when the movement again trended towards the West. In a generation or two, all, whether their forefathers were English, Scotch, Irish, or, as was often the case, German and Huguenot, were welded into one people; and in a very short time the stern and hard surroundings of their life had hammered this people into a peculiar and characteristically American type, which to this day remains almost unchanged. In their old haunts we still see the same tall, gaunt men, with strongly marked faces and saturnine, resolute eyes; men who may pass half their days in listless idleness, but who are also able to show on occasion the fiercest intensity of purpose and the most sustained energy of action. We see them, moreover, in many places, even across to the Pacific coast and down to the Rio Grande. For after thronging through the gaps and passes of the Appalachians, and penetrating the forest region to the outskirts of the treeless country beyond, the whilom mountaineers and woodsmen, the wielders of the axe and rifle, then streamed off far to the West and South and even to the Northwest, their lumbering, white-topped wagons being, even to the present moment, a familiar sight to those who travel over the prairies and the great plains; while it is their descendants who, in the saddle instead of afoot, and with rope and revolver instead of axe and rifle, now form the bulk of the reckless horsemen who spend their lives in guarding the wandering cattle herds that graze over the vast, arid plains of the "Far West."

The method of settlement of these states of the Mississippi valley had nothing whatever in common with the way in which California and the Australian colonies were suddenly filled up by the promiscuous overflow of a civilized population, which had practically no fear of any resistance from the stunted and scanty native races. It was far more closely akin to the tribe movements of the Germanic peoples in time past; to that movement, for example, by which the Juttish and Low Dutch sea-thieves on the coast of Britain worked their way inland at the cost of the Cymric Celts. The early settlers of the territory lying immediately west of the Alleghanies were all of the same kind; they were in search of homes, not of riches, and their actions were planned accordingly, except in so far as they were influenced by mere restless love of adventure and excitement. Individuals and single families, of course, often started off by themselves; but for the most part the men moved in bands, with their wives and their children, their cattle and their few household goods; each settler being from the necessity of the case also a fighter, ready, and often forced, to do desperate battle in defense of himself and his family. Where such a band or little party settled, there would gradually grow up a village or small town; for instance, where those renowned pioneers and heroes of the backwoods, Boone and Harrod, first formed permanent settlements after they had moved into Kentucky, now stand the towns of Boonsboro and Harrodsburg.

The country whither these settlers went was not one into which timid men would willingly venture, and the founders of the West were perforce men of stern stuff, who from the very beginning formed a most warlike race. It is impossible to understand aright the social and political life of the section, unless we keep prominently before our minds that it derived its distinguishing traits largely from the extremely militant character acquired by all the early settlers during the long drawn out warfare in which the first two generations were engaged. The land was already held by powerful Indian tribes and confederacies, who waged war after war, of the most ferocious and bloody character, against the men of the border, in the effort to avert their inevitable doom, or at least to stem for the time being the invasion of the swelling tide of white settlement. At the present time, when an Indian uprising is a matter chiefly of annoyance, and dangerous only to scattered, outlying settlers, it is difficult to realize the formidable nature of the savage Indian wars waged at the end of the last and the beginning of the present centuries. The red nations were then really redoubtable enemies, able to send into the field thousands of well-armed warriors, whose ferocious bravery and skill rendered them quite as formidable antagonists as trained European soldiers would have been. Warfare with them did not affect merely outlying farms or hamlets; it meant a complete stoppage of the white movement westward, and great and imminent danger even to the large communities already in existence; a state of things which would have to continue until the armies raised among the pioneers were able, in fair shock of battle, to shatter the strength of their red foes. The victories of Wayne and Harrison were conditions precedent to the opening of the Ohio valley; Kentucky was won by a hundred nameless and bloody fights, whose heroes, like Shelby and Sevier, afterwards rose to prominent rank in civil life; and it was only after a hard-fought campaign and slaughtering victories that the Tennesseeans were able to break the power of the great Creek confederacy, which was thrust in between them and what were at that time the French and Spanish lands lying to the south and southwest.

The founders of our Western States were valiant warriors as well as hardy pioneers, and from the very first their fighting was not confined to uncivilized foes. It was they who at King's Mountain slew gallant Ferguson, and completely destroyed his little army; it was from their ranks that most of Morgan's men were recruited, when that grizzled old bush-fighter smote Tarleton so roughly at the battle of the Cowpens. These two blows crippled Cornwallis, and were among the chief causes of his final overthrow. At last, during the War of 1812, there was played out the final act in the military drama of which the West had been the stage during the lifetime of a generation. For this war had a twofold aspect: on the sea-board it was regarded as a contest for the rights of our sailors and as a revolt against Great Britain's domineering insolence; west of the mountains, on the other hand, it was simply a renewal on a large scale of the Indian struggles, all the red-skinned peoples joining together in a great and last effort to keep the lands which were being wrested from them; and there Great Britain's part was chiefly that of ally to the savages, helping them with her gold and with her well-drilled mercenary troops. The battle of the Thames is memorable rather because of the defeat and death of Tecumseh, than because of the flight of Proctor and the capture of his British regulars; and for the opening of the Southwest the ferocious fight at the Horseshoe Bend was almost as important as the far more famous conflict of New Orleans.

The War of 1812 brought out conspicuously the solidarity of interest in the West. The people there were then all pretty much of the same blood; and they made common cause against outsiders in the military field exactly as afterwards they for some time acted together politically. Further eastward, on the Niagara frontier, the fighting was done by the troops of New York and New England, unassisted by the Southern States; and in turn the latter had to shift for themselves when Washington was burned and Baltimore menaced. It was far otherwise in the regions lying beyond the Appalachians. Throughout all the fighting in the Northwest, where Ohio was the state most menaced, the troops of Kentucky formed the bulk of the American army, and it was the charge of their mounted riflemen which at a blow won the battle of the Thames. Again, on that famous January morning, when it seemed as if the fair Creole city was already in Packenham's grasp, it was the wild soldiery of Tennessee who, lolling behind their mud breastworks, peered out through the lifting fog at the scarlet array of the English veterans, as the latter, fresh from their long and unbroken series of victories over the best troops of Europe, advanced, for the first time, to meet defeat.

This solidarity of interest and feeling on the part of the trans-Appalachian communities is a factor often not taken into account in relating the political history of the early part of this century; most modern writers (who keep forgetting that the question of slavery was then not one tenth as absorbing as it afterwards became) apparently deeming that the line of demarkation between North and South was at that period, as it has since in reality become, as strongly defined west of the mountains as east of them. That such was not the case was due to several different causes. The first comers into Tennessee and Kentucky belonged to the class of so-called poor whites, who owned few or no slaves, and who were far less sectionally southern in their feelings than were the rich planters of the low, alluvial plains towards the coast of the Atlantic; and though a slave-owning population quickly followed the first pioneers, yet the latter had imprinted a stamp on the character of the two states which was never wholly effaced,—as witness the tens of thousands of soldiers which both, even the more southern of the two, furnished to the Union army in the Civil War.

If this immigration made Kentucky and Tennessee, and afterwards Missouri, less distinctively Southern in character than the South Atlantic States, it at the same time, by furnishing the first and for some time the most numerous element in the population of the states north of the Ohio, made the latter less characteristically Northern than was the case with those lying east of them. Up to 1810 Indiana kept petitioning Congress to allow slavery within her borders; Illinois, in the early days, felt as hostile towards Massachusetts as did Missouri. Moreover, at first the Southern States west of the mountains greatly outweighed the Northern, both in numbers and importance.

Thus several things came about. In the first place, all the communities across the Alleghanies originally felt themselves to be closely knit together by ties of blood, sentiment, and interest; they felt that they were, taking them altogether, Western as opposed to Eastern. In the next place, they were at first Southern rather than Northern in their feeling. But, in the third place, they were by no means so extremely Southern as were the Southern Atlantic States. This was the way in which they looked at themselves; and this was the way in which at that time others looked at them. In our day Kentucky is regarded politically as being simply an integral portion of the solid South; but the greatest of her sons, Clay, was known to his own generation, not as a Southern statesman, but as "Harry of the West." Of the two presidents, Harrison and Taylor, whom the Whigs elected, one lived in Ohio and one in Louisiana; but both were chosen simply as Western men, and, as a matter of fact, both were born in Virginia. Andrew Jackson's victory over Adams was in some slight sense a triumph of the South over the North, but it was far more a triumph of the West over the East. Webster's famous sneer at old Zachary Taylor was aimed at him as a "frontier colonel;" in other words, though Taylor had a large plantation in Louisiana, Webster, and many others besides, looked upon him as the champion of the rough democracy of the West rather than as the representative of the polished slave-holders of the South.

Thus, during the first part of this century, the term "Western" was as applicable to the states lying south of the Ohio as to those lying north of it. Moreover, at first the Central, or, as they were more usually termed, the Border States, were more populous and influential than were those on either side of them, and so largely shaped the general tone of Western feeling. While the voters in these states, whether Whigs or Democrats, accepted as their leaders men like Clay in Kentucky, Benton in Missouri, and Andrew Jackson in Tennessee, it could be taken for granted that on the whole they felt for the South against the North, but much more for the West against the East, and most strongly of all for the Union as against any section whatsoever. Many influences came together to start and keep alive this feeling; but one, more potent than all the others combined, was working steadily, and with ever-increasing power, against it; and when slavery finally brought about a break between the Northern and Southern States of the West as complete as that in the East, then the Democrats of the stamp of Jackson and Benton disappeared as completely from public life as did the Whigs of the stamp of Clay.

Benton's long political career can never be thoroughly understood unless it is kept in mind that he was primarily a Western and not a Southern statesman; and it owes its especial interest to the fact that during its continuance the West first rose to power, acting as a unit, and to the further fact that it was brought to a close by the same causes which soon afterwards broke up the West exactly as the East was already broken. Benton was not one of the few statesmen who have left the indelible marks of their own individuality upon our history; but he was, perhaps, the most typical representative of the statesmanship of the Middle West at the time when the latter gave the tone to the political thought of the entire Mississippi valley. The political school which he represented came to its fullest development in the so-called Border States of Kentucky, Tennessee, and Missouri, and swayed the destinies of the West so long as the states to the north as well as the states to the south were content to accept the leadership of those that lay between them. It came to an end and disappeared from sight when people north of the Ohio at last set up their own standard, and when, after some hesitation, the Border States threw in their lot with the other side and concluded to follow the Southern communities, which they had hitherto led. Benton was one of those public men who formulate and express, rather than shape, the thought of the people who stand behind them and whom they represent. A man of strong intellect and keen energy, he was for many years the foremost representative of at least one phase of that thought; being, also, a man of high principle and determined courage, when a younger generation had grown up and the bent of the thought had changed, he declined to change with it, bravely accepting political defeat as the alternative, and going down without flinching a hair's breadth from the ground on which he had always stood.

To understand his public actions as well as his political ideas and principles it is, of course, necessary to know at least a little of the men among whom he lived and from whom he sprang: the men who were the first of our people to press out beyond the limits of the thirteen old states; who filled Kentucky, Tennessee, Arkansas, and Missouri, and who for so long a time were the dominant class all through the West, until, at last, the flood of Northeastern immigration completely swamped their influence north of the Ohio, while along the Gulf coast the political control slipped from their hands into the grasp of the great planter class.

The wood-choppers, game-hunters, and Indian-fighters, who first came over the mountains, were only the forerunners of the more regular settlers who followed them; but these last had much the same attributes as their predecessors. For many years after the settlements were firmly rooted, the life of the settlers was still subject to all the perils of the wilderness. Above all, the constant warfare in which they were engaged for nearly thirty-five years, and which culminated in the battle of New Orleans, left a deep and lasting imprint on their character. Their incessant wars were waged almost wholly by the settlers themselves, with comparatively little help from the federal government, and with hardly any regular troops as allies. A backwoods levy, whether raised to meet an Indian inroad or to march against the disciplined armies of the British, was merely a force of volunteers, made up from among the full-grown male settlers, who were induced to join either from motives of patriotism, or from love of adventure, or because they felt that their homes and belongings were in danger from which they could only extricate them by their own prowess. Every settler thus became more or less of a soldier, was always expert with the rifle, and was taught to rely upon his own skill and courage for his protection. But the military service in which he was from time to time engaged was of such a lawless kind, and was carried on with such utter absence of discipline, that it did not accustom him in the least to habits of self-command, or render him inclined to brook the exercise of authority by an outsider; so that the Western people grew up with warlike traditions and habits of thought, accustomed to give free rein to their passions, and to take into their own hands the avenging of real or supposed wrongs, but without any of the love for order and for acting in concert with their fellows which characterize those who have seen service in regular armies. On the contrary, the chief effect of this long-continued and harassing Border warfare was to make more marked the sullen and almost defiant self-reliance of the pioneer, and to develop his peculiarly American spirit of individual self-sufficiency, his impatience of outside interference or control, to a degree not known elsewhere, even on this continent. It also gave a distinct military cast to his way of looking at territory which did not belong to him. He stood where he was because he was a conqueror; he had wrested his land by force from its rightful Indian lords; he fully intended to repeat the same feat as soon as he should reach the Spanish lands lying to the west and southwest; he would have done so in the case of French Louisiana if it had not been that the latter was purchased, and was thus saved from being taken by force of arms. This belligerent, or, more properly speaking, piratical way of looking at neighboring territory, was very characteristic of the West, and was at the root of the doctrine of "manifest destiny."

All the early settlers, and most of those who came after them, were poor, living narrow lives fraught with great hardship, and varying between toil and half-aimless roving; even when the conditions of their life became easier it was some time before the influence of their old existence ceased to make itself felt in their way of looking at things. The first pioneers were, it is true, soon followed by great slave-owners; and by degrees there grew up a clan of large landed proprietors and stock-raisers, akin to the planter caste which was so all-powerful along the coast; but it was never relatively either so large or so influential as the latter, and was not separated from the rest of the white population by anything like so wide a gap as that which, in the Southern Atlantic and Gulf States, marked the difference between the rich growers of cotton, rice, and sugar, and the squalid "poor whites" or "crackers."

The people of the Border States were thus mainly composed of small land-owners, scattered throughout the country; they tilled their small farms for themselves, were hewers of their own wood, and drawers of their own water, and for generations remained accustomed to and skillful in the use of the rifle. The pioneers of the Middle West were not dwellers in towns; they kept to the open country, where each man could shift for himself without help or hindrance from his neighbors, scorning the irksome restraints and the lack of individual freedom of city life. They built but few cities of any size; the only two really important ones of whose inhabitants they formed any considerable part, St. Louis and New Orleans, were both founded by the French long before our people came across the mountains into the Mississippi valley. Their life was essentially a country life, alike for the rich and for the bulk of the population. The few raw frontier towns and squalid, straggling villages were neither seats of superior culture nor yet centres for the distribution of educated thought, as in the North. Large tracts of land remained always populated by a class of backwoodsmen differing but little from the first comers. Such was the district from which grand, simple old Davy Crockett went to Washington as a Whig congressman; and perhaps there was never a quainter figure in our national legislature than that of the grim old rifleman, who shares with Daniel Boone the honor of standing foremost in the list of our mighty hunters. Crockett and his kind had little in common with the men who ruled supreme in the politics of most of the Southern States; and even at this day many of their descendants in the wooded mountain land are Republicans; for when the Middle States had lost the control of the West, and when those who had hitherto followed such leaders as Jackson, Clay, and Benton, drifted with the tide that set so strongly to the South, it was only the men of the type of dogged, stubborn old Crockett who dared to make head against it. But, indeed, one of the characteristics of the people with whom we are dealing was the slowness and suspicion with which they received a new idea, and the tenacity with which they clung to one that they had at last adopted.

They were above all a people of strong, virile character, certain to make their weight felt either for good or for evil. They had many virtues which can fairly be called great, and their faults were equally strongly marked. They were not a thrifty people, nor one given to long-sustained, drudging work; there were not then, nor are there now, to be found in this land such comfortable, prosperous homes and farms as those which dot all the country where dwell the men of Northeastern stock. They were not, as a rule, even ordinarily well educated; the public school formed no such important feature in their life as it did in the life of their fellow-citizens farther north. They had narrow, bitter prejudices and dislikes; the hard and dangerous lives they had led had run their character into a stern and almost forbidding mould. They valued personal prowess very highly, and respected no man who did not possess the strongest capacity for self-help, and who could not shift for himself in any danger. They felt an intense, although perhaps ignorant, pride in and love for their country, and looked upon all the lands hemming in the United States as territory which they or their children should some day inherit; for they were a race of masterful spirit, and accustomed to regard with easy tolerance any but the most flagrant violations of law. They prized highly such qualities as courage, loyalty, truth, and patriotism, but they were, as a whole, poor, and not over-scrupulous of the rights of others, nor yet with the nicest sense of money obligations; so that the history of their state legislation affecting the rights of debtor and creditor, whether public or private, in hard times, is not pleasant reading for an American who is proud of his country. Their passions, once roused, were intense, and if they really wished anything they worked for it with indomitable persistency. There was little that was soft or outwardly attractive in their character: it was stern, rude, and hard, like the lives they led; but it was the character of those who were every inch men, and who were Americans through to the very heart's core.

In their private lives their lawless and arrogant freedom and lack of self-restraint produced much gross licentiousness and barbarous cruelty; and every little frontier community could tell its story of animal savagery as regards the home relations of certain of its members. Yet in spite of this they, as a whole, felt the family ties strongly, and in the main had quite a high standard of private morality. Many of them, at any rate, were, according to their lights, deeply and sincerely religious; though even their religion showed their strong, coarse-fibred, narrow natures. Episcopalianism was the creed of the rich slave-owner, who dwelt along the sea-board; but the Western settlers belonged to some one or other of the divisions of the great Methodist and Baptist churches. They were as savagely in earnest about this as about everything else; meekness, mildness, broad liberality, and gentle tolerance of difference in religious views were not virtues they appreciated. They were always ready to do battle for their faith, and, indeed, had to do it, as it was quite a common amusement for the wilder and more lawless members of the community to try to break up by force the great camp-meetings, which formed so conspicuous a feature in the social and religious life of the country. For even irreligion took the form of active rebellion against God, rather than disbelief in his existence.

Physically they were, and are, especially in Kentucky, the finest members of our race; an examination of the statistics relating to the volunteers in the Civil War shows that the natives of no other state, and the men from no foreign country whatsoever, came up to them in bodily development.

Such a people, in choosing men to represent them in the national councils, would naturally pay small heed to refined, graceful, and cultivated statesmanship; their allegiance would be given to men of abounding vitality, of rugged intellect, and of indomitable will. No better or more characteristic possessor of these attributes could be imagined than Thomas Benton.

CHAPTER II.

BENTON'S EARLY LIFE AND ENTRY INTO THE SENATE.

Thomas Hart Benton was born on March 14, 1782, near Hillsborough, in Orange County, North Carolina,—the same state that fifteen years before, almost to a day, had seen the birth of the great political chief whose most prominent supporter he in after life became. Benton, however, came of good colonial stock; and his early surroundings were not characterized by the squalid poverty that marked Jackson's, though the difference in the social condition of the two families was of small consequence on the frontier, where caste was, and is, almost unknown, and social equality is not a mere figure of speech—particularly it was not so at that time in the Southwest, where there were no servants, except black slaves, and where even what in the North would be called "hired help" was almost an unknown quantity.

Benton's father, who was a lawyer in good standing at the North Carolina bar, died when the boy was very young, leaving him to be brought up by his Virginian mother. She was a woman of force, and, for her time, of much education. She herself began the training of her son's mind, studying with him history and biography, while he also, of course, had access to his father's law library. The home in which he was brought up was, for that time and for that part of the country, straightlaced; his mother, though a Virginian, had many traits which belonged rather to the descendants of the Puritans, and possessed both their strength of character and their austerely religious spirit. Although living in a roistering age, among a class peculiarly given to all the coarser kinds of pleasure, and especially to drink and every form of gambling, she nevertheless preserved the most rigid decorum and morality in her own household, frowning especially upon all intemperance, and never permitting a pack of cards to be found within her doors. She was greatly beloved and respected by the son, whose mind she did so much to mould, and she lived to see him become one of the foremost statesmen of the country.

Young Benton was always fond of reading. He began his studies at home, and continued them at a grammar school taught by a young New Englander of good ability, a very large proportion of the school-teachers of the country then coming from New England; indeed, school-teachers and peddlers were, on the whole, the chief contributions made by the Northeast to the *personnel* of the new Southwest. Benton then began a course at Chapel Hill, the University of North Carolina, but broke off before completing it, as his mother decided to move her family westward to the almost unbroken wilderness near Nashville, Tennessee, where his father had left them a large tract of land. But he was such an insatiable student and reader that he rapidly acquired a very extensive knowledge, not only of law, but of history and even of Latin and English literature, and thus became a well-read and cultivated, indeed a learned, man; though his frequent displays of learning and knowledge were sometimes marked by a trace of that self-complacent, amusing pedantry so apt to characterize a really well-educated man who lives in a community in which he believes, and with which he has thoroughly identified himself, but whose members are for the most part below the average in mental cultivation.

The Bentons founded a little town, named after them, and in which, of course, they took their position as leaders and rich landed proprietors. It lay on the very outskirts of the Indian country; indeed, the great war trail of the Southern Indians led right through the settlement, and they at all times swarmed around it. The change from the still somewhat rude civilization of North Carolina to the wildness on the border was far less abrupt and startling then than would be the case under similar circumstances now, and the Bentons soon identified themselves completely with the life and interests of the people around them. They even abandoned the Episcopalianism of their old home, and became Methodists, like their neighbors. Young Benton himself had his hands full, at first, in attending to his great backwoods farm, tilled by slaves, and in pushing the growth of the settlement by building first a rude log school-house (he himself taught school at one time, while studying law), and a meeting-house of the same primitive construction, then mills, roads, bridges, and so forth. The work hardened and developed him, and he readily enough turned into a regular frontiersman of the better and richer sort. The neighboring town of Nashville was a raw, pretentious place, where horse-racing, cock-fighting, gambling, whiskey-drinking, and the various coarse vices which masquerade as pleasures in frontier towns, all throve in rank luxuriance. It was somewhat of a change from Benton's early training, but he took to it kindly, and though never a vicious or debauched man, he bore his full share in the savage brawls, the shooting and stabbing affrays, which went to make up one of the leading features in the excessively unattractive social life of the place and epoch.

At that time dueling prevailed more or less throughout the United States, and in the South and West to an extent never before or since attained. On the frontier, not only did every man of spirit expect now and then to be called on to engage in a duel, but he also had to make up his mind to take occasional part in bloody street-fights. Tennessee, the state where Benton then had his home, was famous for the affrays that took place within its borders; and that they were common enough among the people at large may be gathered from the fact that they were of continual occurrence among judges, high state officials, and in the very legislature itself, where senators and assemblymen were always becoming involved in undignified rows and foolish squabbles, apparently without fear of exciting any unfavorable comment, as witness

Davy Crockett's naive account of his early experiences as a backwoods member of the Tennessee assembly. Like Jackson, Benton killed his man in a duel. This was much later, in 1817, when he was a citizen of Missouri. His opponent was a lawyer named Lucas. They fought twice, on Bloody Island, near St. Louis. On the first occasion both were wounded; on the second Lucas was killed. The latter came of a truculent family. A recent biographer of his father, Judge John R. Lucas, remarks, with refreshing unconsciousness of the grotesque humor of the chronicle: "This gentleman was one of the most remarkable men who ever settled west of the Mississippi River.... Towards the close of his life Judge Lucas became melancholy and dejected— the result of domestic affliction, for six of his sons met death by violence." One feels curious to know how the other sons died.

But the most famous of Benton's affrays was that with Jackson himself, in 1813. This rose out of a duel of laughable rather than serious character, in which Benton's brother was worsted by General Carroll, afterwards one of Jackson's lieutenants at New Orleans. The encounter itself took place between the Benton brothers on one side, and on the other, Jackson, General Coffee, also of New Orleans fame, and another friend. The place was a great rambling Nashville inn, and the details were so intricate that probably not even the participants themselves knew exactly what had taken place, while all the witnesses impartially contradicted each other and themselves. At any rate, Jackson was shot and Benton was pitched headlong down-stairs, and all the other combatants were more or less damaged; but it ended in Jackson being carried off by his friends, leaving the Bentons masters of the field, where they strutted up and down and indulged in a good deal of loud bravado. Previous to this Benton and Jackson had been on the best of terms, and although there was naturally a temporary break in their friendship, yet it proved strong enough in the end to stand even such a violent wrench as that given by this preposterously senseless and almost fatal brawl. They not only became completely reconciled, but eventually even the closest and warmest of personal and political friends; for Benton was as generous and forgiving as he was hot-tempered, and Jackson's ruder nature was at any rate free from any small meanness or malice.

In spite of occasional interludes of this kind, which must have given a rather ferocious fillip to his otherwise monotonous life, Benton completed his legal studies, was admitted to the bar, and began to practice as a frontier lawyer at Franklin. Very soon, however, he for the first time entered the more congenial field of politics, and in 1811 served a single term in the lower house of the Tennessee legislature. Even thus early he made his mark. He had a bill passed introducing the circuit system into the state judiciary, a reform of much importance, especially to the poorer class of litigants; and he also introduced, and had enacted into a law, a bill providing that a slave should have the same right to the full benefit of a jury trial as would a white man suffering under the same accusation. This last measure is noteworthy as foreshadowing the position which Benton afterwards took in national politics, where he appeared as a slave-holder, it is true, but as one of the most enlightened and least radical of his class. Its passage also showed the tendency of Southern opinion at the time, which was undoubtedly in the direction of bettering the condition of the blacks, though the events of the next few years produced such a violent revulsion of feeling concerning the negro race that this current of public opinion was completely reversed. Benton, however, was made of sturdy stuff, and as he grew older his views on the question did not alter as did those of most of his colleagues.

Shortly after he left the legislature the War of 1812 broke out, and its events impressed on Benton another of what soon became his cardinal principles. The war was brought on by the South and West, the Democrats all favoring it, while the Federalists, forming the then anti-Democratic party, especially in the Northeast, opposed it; and finally their more extreme members, at the famous Hartford Convention, passed resolutions supposed to tend towards the dissolution of the Union, and which brought upon the party the bitter condemnation of their antagonists. Says Benton himself: "At the time of its first appearance the right of secession was repulsed and repudiated by the Democracy generally.... The leading language in respect to it south of the Potomac was that no state had a right to withdraw from the Union, ... and that any attempt to dissolve it, or to obstruct the action of constitutional laws, was treason. If since that time political parties and sectional localities have exchanged attitudes on this question, it cannot alter the question of right." For, having once grasped an idea and made it his own, Benton clung to it with unyielding tenacity, no matter whether it was or was not abandoned by the majority of those with whom he had been in the habit of acting.

Thus early Benton's political character became moulded into the shape which it ever afterwards retained. He was a slave-holder, but as advanced as a slave-holder could be; he remained to a certain extent a Southerner, but his Southernism was of the type prevalent immediately after the Revolution, and not of the kind that came to the fore prior to the Rebellion. He was much more a Westerner in his feelings, and more than all else he was emphatically a Union man.

Like every other hot spirit of the West—and the West was full of little but hot spirits—Benton heartily favored the War of 1812. He served as a colonel of volunteers under Jackson, but never saw actual fighting, and his short term of soldiership was of no further account than to furnish an excuse to Polk, thirty-five years later, for nominating him commanding general in the time of the Mexican War,—an incident which, as the nomination was rejected, may be regarded as merely ludicrous, the gross impropriety of the act safely defying criticism. He was of genuine use, however, in calling on and exciting the volunteers to come forward; for he was a fluent speaker, of fine presence, and his pompous self-sufficiency was rather admired than otherwise by the frontiersmen, while his force, energy, and earnestness commanded their respect. He also, when Jackson's reckless impetuosity got him into a snarl with the feeble national administration, whose imbecile incapacity to carry on the war became day by day more painfully evident, went to Washington, and there finally extricated his chief by dint of threatening that, if "justice" was not done him, Tennessee would, in future political contests, be found ranged with the administration's foes. For Benton already possessed political influence, and being, like most of his class, anti-Federalist, or Democratic, in sentiment, was therefore of the same party as the people at Washington, and was a man whose representations would have some weight with them.

During his stay in Tennessee Benton's character was greatly influenced by his being thrown into close contact with many of the extraordinary men who then or afterwards made their mark in the strange and picturesque annals of the Southwest. Jackson even thus early loomed up as the greatest and arch-typical representative of his people and his section. The religious bent of the time was shown in the life of the grand, rugged old Methodist, Peter Cartwright, who, in the far-off backwoods, was a preacher and practical exponent of "muscular Christianity" half a century before the day when, under Bishop Selwyn and Charles Kingsley, it became a cult among the most highly civilized classes of England. There was David Crockett, rifleman and congressman, doomed to a tragic and heroic death in that remarkable conflict of which it was said at the time, that "Thermopylæ had its messengers of death, but the Alamo had none;" and there was Houston, who, after a singular and romantic career, became the greatest of the statesmen and soldiers of Texas. It was these men, and their like, who, under the shadow of world-old forests and in the sunlight of the great, lonely plains, wrought out the destinies of a nation and a continent, and who, with their rude war-craft and state-craft, solved problems that, in the importance of their results, dwarf the issues of all European struggles since the day of Waterloo as completely as the Punic wars in their outcome threw into the shade the consequences of the wars waged at the same time between the different Greek monarchies.

Benton, in his mental training, came much nearer to the statesmen of the sea-board, and was far better bred and better educated, than the rest of the men around him. But he was, and was felt by them to be, thoroughly one of their number, and the most able expounder of their views; and it is just because he is so completely the type of a great and important class, rather than because even of his undoubted and commanding ability as a statesman, that his life and public services will always repay study. His vanity and boastfulness were faults which he shared with almost all his people; and, after all, if they overrated the consequence of their own deeds, the deeds, nevertheless, did possess great importance, and their fault was slight compared to that committed by some of us at the present day, who have gone to the opposite extreme and try to belittle the actions of our fathers. Benton was deeply imbued with the masterful, overbearing spirit of the West,—a spirit whose manifestations are not always agreeable, but the possession of which is certainly a most healthy sign of the virile strength of a young community. He thoroughly appreciated that he was helping to shape the future of a country, whose wonderful development is the most important feature in the history of the nineteenth century; the non-appreciation of which fact is in itself sufficient utterly to disqualify any American statesman from rising to the first rank.

It was not in Tennessee, however, that Benton rose to political prominence, for shortly after the close of the war he crossed the Mississippi and made his permanent home in the territory of Missouri. Missouri was then our extreme western outpost, and its citizens possessed the characteristic western traits to an even exaggerated extent. The people were pushing, restless, and hardy; they were lawless and violent to a degree. In spite of the culture and education of some families, society, as a whole, was marked by florid unconventionality and rawness. The general and widespread intemperance of the judges and high officials of state was even more marked than their proclivities for brawling. The lawyers, as usual, furnished the bulk of the politicians; success at the bar depended less upon learning than upon "push" and audacity. The fatal feuds between individuals and families were as frequent and as bloody as among Highland clans a century before. The following quotations are taken at random from a work on the Bench and Bar of Missouri, by an ex-judge of its supreme court: "A man by the name of Hiram K. Turk, and four sons, settled in 1839 near Warsaw, and a personal difficulty occurred between them and a family of the name of Jones, resulting in the death of one or two. The people began to take sides with one or the other, and finally a general outbreak took place, in which many were killed, resulting in a general reign of terror and of violence beyond the power of the law to subdue." The social annals of this pleasant town of Warsaw could not normally have been dull; in 1844, for instance, they were enlivened by Judge Cherry and Senator Major fighting to the death on one of its principal streets, the latter being slain. The judges themselves were by no means bigoted in their support of law and order. "In those days it was common for people to settle their quarrels during court week.... Judge Allen took great delight in these exhibitions, and would at any time adjourn his court to witness one.... He (Allen) always traveled with a holster of large pistols in front of his saddle, and a knife with a blade at least a foot long." Hannibal Chollop was no mere creature of fancy; on the contrary, his name was legion, and he flourished rankly in every town throughout the Mississippi valley. But, after all, this ruffianism was really not a whit worse in its effects on the national character than was the case with certain of the "universal peace" and "non-resistance" developments in the Northeastern States; in fact, it was more healthy. A class of professional non-combatants is as hurtful to the real, healthy growth of a nation as is a class of fire-eaters; for a weakness or folly is nationally as bad as a vice, or worse; and, in the long run, a Quaker may be quite as undesirable a citizen as is a duelist. No man who is not willing to bear arms and to fight for his rights can give a good reason why he should be entitled to the privilege of living in a free community. The decline of the militant spirit in the Northeast during the first half of this century was much to be regretted. To it is due, more than to any other cause, the undoubted average individual inferiority of the Northern compared to the Southern troops; at any rate, at the beginning of the great war of the Rebellion. The Southerners, by their whole mode of living, their habits, and their love of out-door sports, kept up their warlike spirit; while in the North the so-called upper classes developed along the lines of a wealthy and timid bourgeoisie type, measuring everything by a mercantile standard (a peculiarly debasing one if taken purely by itself), and submitting to be ruled in local affairs by low foreign mobs, and in national matters by their arrogant Southern kinsmen. The militant spirit of these last certainly stood them in good stead in the Civil War. The world has never seen better soldiers than those who followed Lee; and their leader will undoubtedly rank as without any exception the very greatest of all the great captains that the English-speaking peoples have brought forth—and this, although the last and chief of his antagonists may himself claim to stand as the full equal of Marlborough and Wellington.

The other Western States still kept touch on the old colonial communities of the sea-coast, having a second or alternative outlet through Louisiana, newly acquired by the United States, it is true, but which was nevertheless an old settled land. Missouri, however, had lost all connection with the sea-coast, and though, through her great river towns, swarming with raftsmen and flat-boatmen, she drove her main and most thriving trade with the other Mississippi cities, yet her restless and adventure-loving citizens were already seeking other outlets for their activity, and were establishing trade relations with the Mexicans; being thus the earliest among our people to come into active contact with the Hispano-Indian race from whom we afterwards wrested so large a part of their inheritance. Missouri was thrust out beyond the Mississippi into the vast plains-country of the Far West, and except on the river-front was completely isolated, being flanked on every side by great stretches of level wilderness, inhabited by roaming tribes of warlike Indians. Thus for the first time the borderers began to number in their ranks plainsmen as well as backwoodsmen. In such a community there were sure to be numbers of men anxious to take part in any enterprise that united the chance of great pecuniary gain with the certainty of even greater personal risk, and both these conditions were fulfilled in the trading expeditions pushed out from Missouri across the trackless wastes lying between it and the fringe of Mexican settlements on the Rio del Norte. The route followed by these caravans, which brought back furs and precious metals, soon became famous under the name of the Santa Fé trail; and the story of the perils, hardships, and gains of the adventurous traders who followed it would make one of the most striking chapters of American history.

Among such people Benton's views and habits of thought became more markedly Western and ultra-American than ever, especially in regard to our encroachments upon the territory of neighboring powers. The general feeling in the West upon this last subject afterwards crystallized into what became known as the "Manifest Destiny" idea, which, reduced to its simplest terms, was: that it was our manifest destiny to swallow up the land of all adjoining nations who were too weak to withstand us; a theory that forthwith obtained immense popularity among all statesmen of easy international morality. It cannot be too often repeated that no one can understand even the domestic, and more especially the foreign, policy of Benton and his school without first understanding the surroundings amidst which they had been brought up and the people whose chosen representatives they were. Recent historians, for instance, always speak as if our grasping after territory in the Southwest was due solely to the desire of the Southerners to acquire lands out of which to carve new slave-holding states, and as if it was merely a move in the interests of the slave-power. This is true enough so far as the motives of Calhoun, Tyler, and the other public leaders of the Gulf and southern sea-board states were concerned. But the hearty Western support given to the movement was due to entirely different causes, the chief among them being the fact that the Westerners honestly believed themselves to be indeed created the heirs of the earth, or at least of so much of it as was known by the name of North America, and were prepared to struggle stoutly for the immediate possession of their heritage.

One of Benton's earliest public utterances was in regard to a matter which precisely illustrates this feeling. It was while Missouri was still a territory, and when Benton, then a prominent member of the St. Louis bar, had by his force, capacity, and power as a public speaker already become well known among his future constituents. The treaty with Spain, by which we secured Florida, was then before the Senate, which body had to consider it several times, owing to the dull irresolution and sloth of the Spanish government in ratifying it. The bounds it gave us were far too narrow to suit the more fiery Western spirits, and these cheered Benton to the echo when he attacked it in public with fierce vehemence. "The magnificent valley of the Mississippi is ours, with all its fountains, springs, and floods; and woe to the statesman who shall undertake to surrender one drop of its water, one inch of its soil to any foreign power." So he said, his words ringing with the boastful confidence so well liked by the masterful men of the West, strong in their youth, and proudly conscious of their strength. The treaty was ratified in the Senate, nevertheless, all the old Southern States favoring it, and the only votes at any stage recorded against it being of four Western senators, coming respectively from Ohio, Kentucky, Tennessee, and Louisiana. So that in 1818, at any rate, the desire for territorial aggrandizement at the expense of Maine or Mexico was common to the West as a whole, both to the free and the slave states, and was not exclusively favored by the Southerners. The only effect of Benton's speech was to give rise to the idea that he was hostile to the Southern and Democratic administration at Washington, and against this feeling he had to contend in the course of his successful candidacy for the United States senatorship the following year, when Missouri was claiming admittance to the Union.

It was in reference to this matter of admitting Missouri that the slavery question for the first time made its appearance in national politics, where it threw everything into confusion and for the moment overshadowed all else; though it vanished almost as quickly as it had appeared, and did not again come to the front for several years. The Northerners, as a whole, desiring to "restrict" the growth of slavery and the slave-power, demanded that Missouri, before being admitted as a state, should abolish slavery within her boundaries. The South was equally determined that she should be admitted as a slave state; and for the first time the politicians of the country divided on geographical rather than on party lines, though the division proved but temporary, and was of but little interest except as foreshadowing what was to come a score of years later. Even within the territory itself the same contest was carried on with the violence bred by political conflicts in frontier states, there being a very respectable "restriction" party, which favored abolition. Benton was himself a slave-holder, and as the question was in no way one between the East and the West, or between the Union as a whole and any part of it, he naturally gave full swing to his Southern feelings, and entered with tremendous vigor into the contest on the anti-restriction side. So successful were his efforts, and so great was the majority of the Missourians who sympathized with him, that the restrictionists were completely routed and succeeded in electing but one delegate to the constitutional convention. In Congress the matter was finally settled by the passage of the famous Missouri Compromise bill, a measure Southern in its origin, but approved at the time by many if not most Northerners, and disapproved by not a few Southerners. Benton heartily believed in it, announcing somewhat vaguely that he was "equally opposed to slavery agitation and to slavery extension." By its terms Missouri was admitted as a slave state, while slavery was abolished in all the rest of the old province of Louisiana lying north and west of it and north of the parallel of 36° 30'. Owing to an objectionable clause in its Constitution, the admission was not fully completed until 1821, and then only through the instrumentality of Henry Clay. But Benton took his seat immediately, and entered on his thirty years' of service in the United States Senate. His appearance in national politics was thus coincident with the appearance of the question which, it is true, almost immediately sank out of sight for a period of fifteen years, but which then reappeared to stay for good and to become of progressively absorbing importance, until, combining itself with the still greater question of national unity, it dwarfed all other issues, cleft the West as well as the East asunder, and, as one of its minor results, brought about the political downfall of Benton himself and of his whole school in what were called the Border States.

Before entering the Senate, Benton did something which well illustrates his peculiar uprightness, and the care which he took to keep his public acts free from the least suspicion of improper influence. When he was at the bar in St. Louis, real estate litigation was much the most important branch of legal business. The condition of Missouri land-titles was very mixed, since many of them were based upon the thousands of "concessions" of land made by the old French and Spanish governments, which had been ratified by Congress, but subject to certain conditions which the Creole inhabitants, being ignorant and lawless, had generally failed to fulfill. By an act of Congress these inchoate claims were to be brought before the United States recorder of land titles; and the Missouri bar were divided as to what action should be taken on them, the majority insisting that they should be held void, while Benton headed the opposite party, which was averse to forfeiting property on technical grounds, and advocated the confirmation of every honest claim. Further and important legislation was needed to provide for these claims. Benton, being much the most influential member of the bar who had advocated the confirmation of the claims, and being so able, honest, and energetic, was the favorite counsel of the claimants, and had hundreds of their titles under his professional charge. Of course in such cases the compensation of the lawyer depended solely upon his success; and success to Benton would have meant wealth. Nevertheless, and though his action was greatly to his own pecuniary hurt, the first thing he did when elected senator was to convene his clients, and tell them that henceforth he could have nothing more to do, as their attorney, with the prosecution of their claims, giving as his reason that their success largely depended upon the action of Congress, of which he was now himself a member, so that he was bound to consult, not any private interest, but the good of the community as a whole. He even refused to designate his successor in the causes, saying that he was determined not only to be quite unbiased in acting upon the subject of these claims as senator, but not to have, nor to be suspected of having, any personal interest in the fate of any of them. Many a modern statesman might most profitably copy his sensitiveness.

CHAPTER III.

EARLY YEARS IN THE SENATE.

When Benton took his seat in the United States Senate, Monroe, the last president of the great house of Virginia, was about beginning his second term. He was a courteous, high-bred gentleman, of no especial ability, but well fitted to act as presidential figure-head during the politically quiet years of that era of good feeling which lasted from 1816 till 1824. The Federalist party, after its conduct during the war, had vanished into well-deserved obscurity, and though influences of various sorts were working most powerfully to split the dominant and all-embracing Democracy into factional fragments, these movements had not yet come to a head.

The slavery question, it cannot be too often said, was as yet of little or no political consequence. The violent excitement over the admission of Missouri had subsided as quickly as it had arisen; and though the Compromise bill was of immense importance in itself, and still more as giving a hint of what was to come, it must be remembered that its effect upon general politics, during the years immediately succeeding its passage, was slight. Later on, the slavery question became of such paramount consequence, and so completely identified with the movement for the dissolution of the Union, that it seems impossible for even the best of recent historians of American politics to understand that such was not the case at this time. One writer of note even goes so far as to state that "From the night of March 2, 1820, party history is made up without interruption or break of the development of geographical [the context shows this to mean Northern and Southern] parties." There is very little ground for such a sweeping assertion until a considerable time after the date indicated; indeed, it was more than ten years later before any symptom of the development spoken of became at all marked. Until then, parties divided even less on geographical lines than had been the case earlier, during the last years of the existence of the Federalists; and what little division there was had no reference to slavery. Nor was it till nearly a score of years after the passage of the Missouri Compromise bill that the separatist spirit began to identify itself for good with the idea of the maintenance of slavery. Previously to that there had been outbursts of separatist feeling in different states, but always due to entirely different causes. Georgia flared up in hot defiance of the federal government, when the latter rubbed against her on the question of removing the Cherokees from within her borders. But her having negro slaves did not affect her feelings in the least, and her attitude was just such as any Western state with Indians on its frontier is now apt to assume so far as it dares,—such an attitude as Arizona, for example, would at this moment take in reference to the Apaches, if she were able. Slavery was doubtless remotely one of the irritating causes that combined to work South

Carolina up to a fever heat of insanity over the nullification excitement. But in its immediate origin nullification arose from the outcry against the protective tariff, and it is almost as unfair to ascribe it in any way to the influence of slavery as it would be to assign a similar cause for the Virginia and Kentucky resolutions of 1798, or to say that the absence of slavery was the reason for the abortively disloyal agitation in New England, which culminated in the Hartford Convention. The separatist feeling is ingrained in the fibre of our race, and though in itself a most dangerous failing and weakness, is yet merely a perversion and distortion of the defiant and self-reliant independence of spirit which is one of the chief of the race virtues; and slavery was partly the cause and partly merely the occasion of the abnormal growth of the separatist movement in the South. Nor was the tariff question so intimately associated with that of slavery as has been commonly asserted. This might be easily guessed from the fact that the originator and chief advocate of a high tariff himself came from a slave state, and drew many of his warmest supporters from among the slave-holding sugar-planters. Except in the futile discussion over the proposed Panama Congress it was not till Benton's third senatorial term that slavery became of really great weight in politics.

One of the first subjects that attracted Benton's attention in the Senate was the Oregon question, and on this he showed himself at once in his true character as a Western man, proud alike of every part of his country, and as desirous of seeing the West extended in a northerly as in a southerly direction. Himself a slave-holder, from a slave state, he was one of the earliest and most vehement advocates of the extension of our free territory northwards along the Pacific coast. All the country stretching north and south of the Oregon River was then held by the United States in joint possession with Great Britain. But the whole region was still entirely unsettled, and as a matter of fact our British rivals were the only parties in actual occupation. The title to the territory was doubtful, as must always be the case when it rests upon the inaccurate maps of forgotten explorers, or upon the chance landings of stray sailors and traders, especially if the land in dispute is unoccupied and of vast but uncertain extent, of little present value, and far distant from the powers claiming it. The real truth is that such titles are of very little practical value, and are rightly enough disregarded by any nations strong enough to do so. Benton's intense Americanism, and his pride and confidence in his country and in her unlimited capacity for growth of every sort, gifted him with the power to look much farther into the future, as regarded the expansion of the United States, than did his colleagues; and moreover caused him to consider the question from a much more far-seeing and statesmanlike stand-point. The land belonged to no man, and yet was sure to become very valuable; our title to it was not very good, but was probably better than that of any one else. Sooner or later it would be filled with the overflow of our population, and would border on our dominion, and on our dominion alone. It was therefore just, and moreover in the highest degree desirable, that it should be made a part of that dominion at the earliest possible moment. Benton introduced a bill to enable the president to terminate the arrangement with Great Britain and make a definite settlement in our favor; and though the Senate refused to pass it, yet he had the satisfaction of bringing the subject prominently before the people, and, moreover, of outlining the way in which it would have to be and was finally settled. In one of his speeches on the matter he said, using rather highflown language, (for he was unfortunately deficient in sense of humor): "Upon the people of Eastern Asia the establishment of a civilized power on the opposite coast of America could not fail to produce great and wonderful benefits. Science, liberal principles in government, and the true religion might cast their lights across the intervening sea. The valley of the Columbia might become the granary of China and Japan, and an outlet to their imprisoned and exuberant population." Could he have foreseen how, in the future, the Americans of the valley of the Columbia would greet the "imprisoned and exuberant population" of China, he would probably have been more doubtful as to the willingness of the latter empire to accept our standard of the true religion and liberal principles of government. In the course of the same speech he for the first time, and by what was then considered a bold flight of imagination, suggested the possibility of sending foreign ministers to the Oriental nations, to China, Japan, and Persia, "and even to the Grand Turk."

Better success attended a bill he introduced to establish a trading-road from Missouri through the Indian country to New Mexico, which, after much debate, passed both houses and was signed by President Monroe. The road thus marked out and established became, and remained for many years, a great thoroughfare, and among the chief of the channels through which our foreign commerce flowed. Until Benton secured the enactment of this law, so important to the interests and development of the West, the overland trade with Mexico had been carried on by individual effort and at the cost of incalculable hazard, hardship, and risk of life. Mexico, with its gold and silver mines, its strange physical features, its population utterly foreign to us in race, religion, speech, and ways of life, and especially because of the glamour of mystery which surrounded it and partly shrouded it from sight, always dazzled and strongly attracted the minds of the Southwesterners, occupying much the same place in their thoughts that the Spanish Main did in the imagination of England during the reign of Elizabeth. The young men of the Mississippi valley looked upon an expedition with one of the bands of armed traders, who wound their way across Indian-haunted wastes, through deep canyons and over lofty mountain passes, to Santa Fé, Chihuahua, and Sonora, with the same feelings of eager excitement and longing that were doubtless felt by some of their forefathers more than two centuries previously in regard to the cruises of Drake and Hawkins. The long wagon trains or pack trains of the traders carried with them all kinds of goods, but especially cotton, and brought back gold and silver bullion, bales of furs and droves of mules; and, moreover, they brought back tales of lawless adventure, of great gains and losses, of fights against Indians and Mexicans, and of triumphs and privations, which still further inflamed the minds of the Western men. Where they had already gone as traders, who could on occasion fight, they all hoped on some future day to go as warriors, who would acquire gain by their conquests. These hopes were openly expressed, and with very little more idea of there being any right or wrong in the matter than so many Norse Vikings might have felt. The Southwesterners are credited with altogether too complex motives when it is supposed that they were actuated in regard to the conquest of northern Mexico by a desire to provide for additional slave states to offset the growth of the North; their emotions in regard to their neighbor's land were in the main perfectly simple and purely piratical. That the Northeast did not share in the greed for new territory felt by the other sections of the country was due partly to the decline in its militant spirit, (a decline on many accounts sincerely to be regretted,) and partly to its geographical situation, since it adjoined Canada, an unattractive and already well-settled country, jealously guarded by the might of Great Britain.

Another question, on which Benton showed himself to be thoroughly a representative of Western sentiment, was the removal of the Indian tribes. Here he took a most active and prominent part in reporting and favoring the bills, and in advocating the treaties, by which the Indian tribes of the South and West were forced or induced, (for the latter word was very frequently used as a euphemistic synonym of the former,) to abandon great tracts of territory to the whites and to move farther away from the boundaries of their ever-encroaching civilization. Nor was his action wholly limited to the Senate, for it was at his instance that General Clark, at St. Louis, concluded the treaties with the Kansas and Osage tribes, by which the latter surrendered to the United States all the vast territory which they nominally owned west of Missouri and Arkansas, except small reserves for themselves. Benton, as was to be expected, took the frontier view of the Indian question, which, by the way, though often wrong, is much more apt to be right than is the so-called humanitarian or Eastern view. But, so far as was compatible with having the Indians removed, he always endeavored to have them kindly and humanely treated. There was, of course, much injustice and wrong inevitably attendant upon the Indian policy advocated by him, and by the rest of the Southern and Western statesmen; but it is difficult to see what other course could have been pursued with most of the tribes. In the Western States there were then sixty millions of acres of the best land, owned in great tracts by barbarous or half-barbarous Indians, who were always troublesome and often dangerous neighbors, and who did not come in any way under the laws of the states in which they lived. The states thus encumbered would evidently never have been satisfied until all their soil was under their own jurisdiction and open to settlement. The Cherokees had advanced far on the road toward civilization, and it was undoubtedly a cruel grief and wrong to take them away from their homes; but the only alternative would have been to deprive them of much of their land, and to provide for their gradually becoming citizens of the states in which they were. For a movement of this sort the times were not then, and, unfortunately, are not yet ripe.

Much maudlin nonsense has been written about the governmental treatment of the Indians, especially as regards taking their land. For the simple truth is that they had no possible title to most of the lands we took, not even that of occupancy, and at the most were in possession merely by virtue of having butchered the previous inhabitants. For many of its actions towards them the government does indeed deserve the severest criticism; but it has erred quite as often on the side of too much leniency as on the side of too much severity. From the very nature of things, it was wholly impossible that there should not be much mutual wrong-doing and injury in the intercourse between the Indians and ourselves. It was equally out of the question to let them remain as they were, and to bring the bulk of their number up to our standard of civilization with sufficient speed to enable them to accommodate themselves to the changed condition of their surroundings. The policy towards them advocated by Benton, which was much the same as, although more humane than, that followed by most other Western men who have had practically to face the problem, worked harshly in many instances, and was the cause of a certain amount of temporary suffering. But it was infinitely better for the nation, as a whole, and, in the end, was really more just and merciful, than it would have been to attempt following out any of the visionary schemes which the more impracticable Indian enthusiasts are fond of recommending.

It was during Monroe's last term that Henry Clay brought in the first protective tariff bill, as distinguished from tariff bills to raise revenue with protection as an incident only. It was passed by a curiously mixed vote, which hardly indicated any one's future position on the tariff excepting that of Clay himself; Massachusetts, under the lead of Webster, joining hands with the Southern sea-coast states to oppose it, while Tennessee and New York split, and Missouri and Kentucky, together with most of the North, favored it. Benton voted for it, but on the great question of internal improvements he stood out clearly for the views that he ever afterwards held. This was first brought up by the veto, on constitutional grounds, of the Cumberland Road bill, which had previously passed both houses with singular unanimity, Benton's vote being one of the very few recorded against it. In regard to all such matters Benton was strongly in favor of a strict construction of the Constitution and of guarding the rights of the states, in spite of his devoted attachment to the Union. While voting against this bill, and denying the power or the right of the federal government to take charge of improvements which would benefit one state only, Benton was nevertheless careful to reserve to himself the right to support measures for improving national rivers or harbors yielding revenues. The trouble is, that however much the two classes of cases may differ in point of expediency, they overlap so completely that it is wholly impossible to draw a hard and fast line between them, and the question of constitutionality, if waived in the one instance, can scarcely with propriety be raised in the other.

With the close of Monroe's second term the "era of good feeling" came to an end, and the great Democratic-Republican party split up into several fragments, which gradually crystallized round two centres. But in 1824 this process was still incomplete, and the presidential election of that year was a simple scramble between four different candidates,—Jackson, Adams, Clay, and Crawford. Jackson had the greatest number of votes, but as no one had a majority, the election was thrown into the House of Representatives, where the Clay men, inasmuch as their candidate was out of the race, went over to Adams and elected him. Benton at the time, and afterwards in his "Thirty Years' View," inveighed against this choice as being a violation of what he called the "principle demos krateo"—a barbarous phrase for which he had a great fondness, and which he used and misused on every possible occasion, whether in speaking or writing. He insisted that, as Jackson had secured the majority of the electoral vote, it was the duty of the House of Representatives to ratify promptly this "choice of the people." The Constitution expressly provided that this need not be done. So Benton, who on questions of state rights and internal improvements was so pronounced a stickler for a strict construction of the Constitution, here coolly assumed the absurd position that the Constitution was wrong on this particular point, and should be disregarded, on the ground that there was a struggle "between the theory of the Constitution and the democratic principle." His proposition was ridiculous. The "democratic principle" had nothing more to do with the matter than had the law of gravitation. Either the Constitution was or it was not to be accepted as a serious document, that meant something; in the former case the election of Adams was proper in every aspect, in the latter it was unnecessary to have held any election at all.

At this period every one was floundering about in efforts to establish political relations, Benton not less than others; for he had begun the canvass as a supporter of Clay, and had then gone over to Crawford. But at the end he had become a Jacksonian Democrat, and during the rest of his political career he figured as the most prominent representative of the Jacksonian

Democracy in the Senate. Van Buren himself, afterwards Jackson's prime favorite and political heir, was a Crawford man during this campaign.

Adams, after his election, which was owing to Clay's support, gave Clay the position of secretary of state in his cabinet. The affair unquestionably had an unfortunate look, and the Jacksonians, especially Jackson, at once raised a great hue and cry that there had been a corrupt bargain. Benton, much to his credit, refused to join in the outcry, stating that he had good and sufficient reasons—which he gave—to be sure of its falsity; a position which brought him into temporary disfavor with many of his party associates, and which a man who had Benton's ambition and bitter partisanship, without having his sturdy pluck, would have hesitated to take. The assault was directed with especial bitterness against Clay, whom Jackson ever afterwards included in the very large list of individuals whom he hated with the most rancorous and unreasoning virulence. Randolph of Roanoke, the privileged eccentric of the Senate, in one of those long harangues in which he touched upon everybody and everything, except possibly the point at issue, made a rabid onslaught upon the Clay-Adams coalition as an alliance of "the blackleg and the Puritan." Clay, who was susceptible enough to the charge of loose living, but who was a man of rigid honor and rather fond than otherwise of fighting, promptly challenged him, and a harmless interchange of shots took place. Benton was on the field as the friend of both parties, and his account of the affair is very amusing in its description of the solemn, hair-splitting punctilio with which it is evident that both Randolph and many of his contemporaries regarded points of dueling honor, which to us seem either absurd, trivial, or wholly incomprehensible.

Two tolerably well-defined parties now emerged from the chaos of contending politicians; one was the party of the administration, whose members called themselves National Republicans, and later on Whigs; the other was the Jacksonian Democracy. Adams's inaugural address and first message outlined the Whig policy as favoring a protective tariff, internal improvements, and a free construction of the Constitution generally. The Jacksonians accordingly took the opposite side on all these points, partly from principle and partly from perversity. In the Senate they assailed with turgid eloquence every administration measure, whether it was good or bad, very much of their opposition being purely factious in character. There has never been a time when there was more rabid, objectless, and unscrupulous display of partisanship. Benton, little to his credit, was a leader in these purposeless conflicts. The most furious of them took place over the proposed Panama mission. This was a scheme that originated in the fertile brain of Henry Clay, whose Americanism was of a type quite as pronounced as Benton's, and who was always inclined to drag us into a position of hostility to European powers. The Spanish-American States, having succeeded in winning their independence from Spain, were desirous of establishing some principle of concert in action among the American republics as a whole, and for this purpose proposed to hold an international congress at Panama. Clay's fondness for a spirited and spectacular foreign policy made him grasp eagerly at the chance of transforming the United States into the head of an American league of free republics, which would be a kind of cis-Atlantic offset to the Holy Alliance of European despotisms. Adams took up the idea, nominated ministers to the Panama Congress, and gave his reasons for his course in a special message to the Senate. The administration men drew the most rosy and impossible pictures of the incalculable benefits which would be derived from the proposed congress; and the Jacksonians attacked it with an exaggerated denunciation that was even less justified by the facts.

Adams's message was properly open to attack on one or two points; notably in reference to its proposals that we should endeavor to get the Spanish-American States to introduce religious tolerance within their borders. It was certainly an unhappy suggestion that we should endeavor to remove the mote of religious intolerance from our brother's eye while indignantly resenting the least allusion to the beam of slavery in our own. It was on this very point of slavery that the real opposition hinged. The Spanish States had emancipated their comparatively small negro populations, and, as is usually the case with Latin nations, did not have a very strong caste feeling against the blacks, some of whom accordingly had risen to high civic and military rank; and they also proposed to admit to their congress the negro republic of Hayti. Certain of the slave-holders of the South fiercely objected to any such association; and on this occasion Benton for once led and voiced the ultra-Southern feeling on the subject, announcing in his speech that diplomatic intercourse with Hayti should not even be discussed in the senate chamber, and that we could have no association with republics who had "black generals in their armies and mulatto senators in their congresses." But this feeling on the part of the slave-holders against the measure was largely, although not wholly, spurious; and really had less to do with the attitude of the Jacksonian Democrats than had a mere factious opposition to Adams and Clay. This was shown by the vote on the confirmation of the ministers, when the senators divided on party and not on sectional lines. The nominations were confirmed, but not till after such a length of time that the ministers were unable to reach Panama until after the congress had adjourned.

The Oregon question again came up during Adams's term, the administration favoring the renewal of the joint occupation convention, by which we held the country in common with Great Britain. There was not much public feeling in the matter; in the East there was none whatever. But Benton, when he opposed the renewal, and claimed the whole territory as ours, gave expression to the desires of all the Westerners who thought over the subject at all. He was followed by only half a dozen senators, all but one from the West, and from both sides of the Ohio—Illinois, Kentucky, Tennessee, Mississippi; the Northwest and Southwest as usual acting together.

The vote on the protective tariff law of 1828 furnished another illustration of the solidarity of the West. New England had abandoned her free trade position since 1824, and the North went strongly for the new tariff; the Southern sea-coast states, except Louisiana, opposed it bitterly; and the bill was carried by the support of the Western States, both the free and the slave. This tariff bill was the first of the immediate irritating causes which induced South Carolina to go into the nullification movement. Benton's attitude on the measure was that of a good many other men who, in their public capacities, are obliged to appear as protectionists, but who lack his frankness in stating their reasons. He utterly disbelieved in and was opposed to the principle of the bill, but as it had bid for and secured the interest of Missouri by a heavy duty on lead, he felt himself forced to support it; and so he announced his position. He simply went with his state, precisely as did Webster, the latter, in following Massachusetts' change of front and supporting the tariff of 1828, turning a full and complete somersault. Neither the one nor the other was to blame. Free traders are apt to look at the tariff from a sentimental stand-point; but it is in reality purely a business matter, and should be decided solely on grounds of expediency. Political economists have pretty generally agreed that protection is vicious in theory and harmful in practice; but if the majority of the people in interest wish it, and it affects only themselves, there is no earthly reason why they should not be allowed to try the experiment to their hearts' content. The trouble is that it rarely does affect only themselves; and in 1828 the evil was peculiarly aggravated on account of the unequal way in which the proposed law would affect different sections. It purported to benefit the rest of the country, but it undoubtedly worked real injury to the planter states, and there is small ground for wonder that the irritation over it in the region so affected should have been intense.

During Adams's term Benton began his fight for disposing of the public lands to actual settlers at a small cost. It was a move of enormous importance to the whole West; and Benton's long and sturdy contest for it, and for the right of preëmption, entitle him to the greatest credit. He never gave up the struggle, although repulsed again and again, and at the best only partially successful; for he had to encounter much opposition, especially from the short-sighted selfishness of many of the Northeasterners, who wished to consider the public lands purely as sources of revenue. He utterly opposed the then existing system of selling land to the highest bidder—a most hurtful practice; and objected to the establishment of an arbitrary minimum price, which practically kept all land below a certain value out of the market altogether. He succeeded in establishing the preëmption system, and had the system of renting public mines, etc., abolished; and he struggled for the principle of giving land outright to settlers in certain cases. As a whole, his theory of a liberal system of land distribution was undoubtedly the correct one, and he deserves the greatest credit for having pushed it as he did.

CHAPTER IV.

THE ELECTION OF JACKSON, AND THE SPOILS SYSTEM.

In the presidential election of 1828 Jackson and Adams were pitted against each other as the only candidates before the people, and Jackson won an overwhelming victory. The followers of the two were fast developing respectively into Democrats and Whigs, and the parties were hardening and taking shape, while the dividing lines were being drawn more clearly and distinctly. But the contest was largely a personal one, and Jackson's success was due to his own immense popularity more than to any party principles which he was supposed to represent. Almost the entire strength of Adams was in the Northeast; but it is absolutely wrong to assume, because of this fact, that the election even remotely foreshadowed the way in which party lines would be drawn in the coming sectional antagonism over slavery. Adams led Jackson in the two slave states of Maryland and Delaware; and in the free states outside of New England Jackson had an even greater lead over Adams. East of the Alleghanies it may here and there have been taken as in some sort a triumph of the South over the North; but its sectional significance, as far as it had any, really came from its being a victory of the West over the East. Infinitely more important than this was the fact that it represented the overwhelmingly successful upheaval of the most extreme democratic elements in the community.

Until 1828 all the presidents, and indeed almost all the men who took the lead in public life, alike in national and in state affairs, had been drawn from what in Europe would have been called the "upper classes." They were mainly college-bred men of high social standing, as well educated as any in the community, usually rich or at least well-to-do. Their subordinates in office were of much the same material. It was believed, and the belief was acted upon, that public life needed an apprenticeship of training and experience. Many of our public men had been able; almost all had been honorable and upright. The change of parties in 1800, when the Jeffersonian Democracy came in, altered the policy of the government, but not the character of the officials. In that movement, though Jefferson had behind him the mass of the people as the rank and file of his party, yet all his captains were still drawn from among the men in the same social position as himself. The Revolutionary War had been fought under the leadership of the colonial gentry; and for years after it was over the people, as a whole, felt that their interests could be safely intrusted to and were identical with those of the descendants of their revolutionary leaders. The classes in which were to be found almost all the learning, the talent, the business activity, and the inherited wealth and refinement of the country, had also hitherto contributed much to the body of its rulers.

The Jacksonian Democracy stood for the revolt against these rulers; its leaders, as well as their followers, all came from the mass of the people. The majority of the voters supported Jackson because they felt he was one of themselves, and because they understood that his election would mean the complete overthrow of the classes in power and their retirement from the control of the government. There was nothing to be said against the rulers of the day; they had served the country and all its citizens well, and they were dismissed, not because the voters could truthfully allege any wrong-doing whatsoever against them, but solely because, in their purely private and personal feelings and habits of life, they were supposed to differ from the mass of the people. This was such an outrageously absurd feeling that the very men who were actuated by it, or who, like Benton, shaped and guided it, were ashamed to confess the true reason of their actions, and tried to cloak it behind an outcry, as vague and senseless as it was clamorous, against "aristocratic corruption" and other shadowy and spectral evils. Benton even talked loosely of "retrieving the country from the deplorable condition in which the enlightened classes had sunk it," although the country was perfectly prosperous and in its usual state of quiet, healthy growth. On the other hand, the opponents of Jackson indulged in talk almost as wild, and fears even more extravagant than his supporters' hopes; and the root of much of their opposition lay in a concealed but still existent caste antagonism to a man of Jackson's birth and bringing up. In fact, neither side, in spite of all their loud talk of American Republicanism, had yet mastered enough of its true spirit to be able to see that so long as public officers did their whole duty to all classes alike, it was not in the least the affair of their constituents whether they chose to spend their hours of social relaxation in their shirt-sleeves or in dress coats.

The change was a great one; it was not a change of the policy under which the government was managed, as in Jefferson's triumph, but of the men who controlled it. The two great democratic victories had little in common; almost as little as had the two great leaders under whose auspices they were respectively won,—and few men were ever more unlike than the scholarly, timid, and shifty doctrinaire, who supplanted the elder Adams, and the ignorant, headstrong, and straightforward soldier, who was victor over the younger. That the change was the deliberate choice of the great mass of the people, and that it was one for the worse, was then, and has been ever since, the opinion of most thinking men; certainly the public service then took its first and greatest step in that downward career of progressive debasement and deterioration which has only been checked in our own days. But those who would, off-hand, decry the democratic principle on this account would do well to look at the nearly contemporaneous career of the pet heroes of a trans-Atlantic aristocracy before passing judgment. A very charming English historian of our day[1] has compared Wellington with Washington; it would have been far juster to have compared him with Andrew Jackson. Both were men of strong, narrow minds and bitter prejudices, with few statesmanlike qualities, who, for brilliant military services, were raised to the highest civil positions in the gift of the state. The feeling among the aristocratic classes of Great Britain in favor of the Iron Duke was nearly as strong and quite as unreasonable as was the homage paid by their homelier kinsfolk across the Atlantic to Old Hickory. Wellington's military successes were far greater, for he had more chances; but no single feat of his surpassed the remarkable victory won against his ablest lieutenant and choicest troops by a much smaller number of backwoods riflemen under Andrew Jackson. As a statesman Wellington may have done less harm than Jackson, for he had less influence; but he has no such great mark to his credit as the old Tennessean's attitude toward the Nullifiers. If Jackson's election is a proof that the majority is not always right, Wellington's elevation may be taken as showing that the minority, or a fraction thereof, is in its turn quite as likely to be wrong.

This caste antagonism was the distinguishing feature in the election of 1828, and the partially sectional character of the contest was due to the different degree of development the caste spirit had reached in different portions of the Union. In New England wealth was quite evenly distributed, and education and intelligence were nearly universal; so there the antagonism was slight, the bulk of the New England vote being given, as usually before and since, in favor of the right candidate. In the Middle States, on the contrary, the antagonism was very strong. In the South it was of but little political account as between the whites themselves, they all being knit together by the barbarous bond of a common lordship of race; and here the feeling for Jackson was largely derived from the close kinship still felt for the West. In the West itself, where Jackson's great strength lay, the people were still too much on the same plane of thought as well as of material prosperity, and the wealthy and cultivated classes were of too limited extent to admit of much caste feeling against the latter; and, accordingly, instead of hostility to them, the Western caste spirit took the form of hostility to their far more numerous representatives who had hitherto formed the bulk of the political rulers of the East.

New England was not only the most advanced portion of the Union, as regards intelligence, culture, and general prosperity, but was also most disagreeably aware of the fact, and was possessed with a self-conscious virtue that was peculiarly irritating to the Westerners, who knew that they were looked down upon, and savagely resented it on every occasion; and, besides, New England was apt to meddle in affairs that more nearly concerned other localities. Several of Benton's speeches, at this time, show this irritation against the Northeast, and also incidentally bring out the solidarity of interest felt throughout the West. In a long and able speech, favoring the repeal of the iniquitous "salt tax," or high duty on imported salt (a great hobby of his, in which, after many efforts, he was finally successful), he brought out the latter point very strongly, besides complaining of the disproportionate lightness of the burden imposed upon the Northeast by the high tariff, of which he announced himself to be but a moderate adherent. In common with all other Western statesmen, he resented keenly the suspicion with which the Northeast was then only too apt to regard the West, quoting in one of his speeches with angry resentment a prevalent New England sneer at "the savages beyond the Alleghanies." At the time we are speaking of it must be remembered that many even of the most advanced Easterners were utterly incapable of appreciating the almost limitless capacity of their country for growth and expansion, being in this respect far behind their Western brethren; indeed, many regarded the acquisition of any new territory in the West with alarm and regret, as tending to make the Union of such unwieldy size that it would break of its own weight.

Benton was the leading opponent of a proposal, introduced by Senator Foot of Connecticut, to inquire into the expediency of limiting the sales of public lands to such lands as were then in the market. The limitation would have been most injurious to the entire West, which was thus menaced by the action of a New Englander, while Benton appeared as the champion of the whole section, North and South alike, in the speech wherein he strenuously and successfully opposed the adoption of the resolution, and at the same time bitterly attacked the quarter of the country from which it came, as having from the earliest years opposed everything that might advance the interests of the people beyond the Alleghanies. Webster came to the assistance of the mover of the measure in a speech wherein, among other things, he claimed for the North the merit of the passage of the Ordinance of 1787, in relation to the Northwest Territory, and especially of the anti-slavery clause therein contained. But Benton here caught him tripping, and in a very good speech showed that he was completely mistaken in his facts. The debate now, however, completely left the point at issue, taking a bitterly sectional turn, and giving rise to the famous controversy between Hayne, of South Carolina, who for the first time on the floor of the Senate announced the doctrine of nullification, and Webster, who, in response to his antagonist, voiced the feeling of the Union men of the North in that wonderful and magnificent speech known ever since under the name of the "Reply to Hayne," and the calling forth of which will henceforward be Hayne's sole title to fame. Benton, though himself a strong Union and anti-nullification man, was still too excited over the subject-matter of the bill and the original discussion over it to understand that the debate had ranged off upon matters of infinitely greater importance, and entirely failed to realize that he had listened to the greatest piece of oratory of the century. On the contrary, encouraged by his success earlier in the debate, he actually attempted a kind of reply to Webster, attacking him with invective and sarcasm as an alarmist, and taunting him with the memory of the Hartford Convention, which had been held by members of the Federalist party, to which Webster himself had once belonged. Benton afterwards became convinced that Webster's views were by no means those of a mere alarmist, and frankly stated that he had been wrong in his position; but at the time, heated by his original grievance, as a Western man, against New England, he failed entirely to understand the true drift of Hayne's speech. Much of New England's policy to the West was certainly excessively narrow-minded.

Jackson's administration derives a most unenviable notoriety as being the one under which the "spoils system" became, for the first time, grafted on the civil service of the nation; appointments and removals in the public service being made dependent upon political qualifications, and not, as hitherto, upon merit or capacity. Benton, to his honor, always stoutly opposed this system. It is unfair to assert that Jackson was the originator of this method of appointment; but he was certainly its foster-father, and more than any one else is responsible for its introduction into the affairs of the national government. Despite all the Eastern sneers at the "savages" of the West, it was from Eastern men that this most effective method of debauching political life came. The Jacksonian Democrats of the West, when they introduced it into the working of the federal government, simply copied the system which they found already firmly established by their Eastern allies in New York and Pennsylvania. For many years the course of politics throughout the country had been preparing and foreshadowing the advent of the "spoils system." The greatest single stroke in its favor had been done at the instigation of Crawford, when that scheming politician was seeking the presidency, and, to further his ends, he procured the passage by Congress of a law limiting the term of service of all public officials to four years, thus turning out of office all the fifty thousand public servants during each presidential term. This law has never been repealed, every low politician being vitally interested in keeping it as it is, and accordingly it is to be found on the statute-books at the present day; and though it has the company of some other very bad measures, it still remains very much the worst of all, as regards both the evil it has done and that which it is still doing. This four years' limitation law was passed without comment or protest, every one voting in its favor, its probable working not being comprehended in the least. Says Benton, who, with all his colleagues, voted for it: "The object of the law was to pass the disbursing officers every four years under the supervision of the appointing power, for the inspection of their accounts, in order that defaulters might be detected and dropped, while the faithful should be ascertained and continued.... It was found to operate contrary to its intent, and to have become the facile means of getting rid of faithful disbursing officers, instead of retaining them." New York has always had a low political standard, one or the other of its great party and factional organizations, and often both or all of them, being at all times most unlovely bodies of excessively unwholesome moral tone. Aaron Burr introduced the "spoils system" into her state affairs, and his methods were followed and improved upon by Marcy, Wright, Van Buren, and all the "Albany Regency." In 1829 these men found themselves an important constituent portion of the winning party, and immediately, by the help of the only too willing Jackson, proceeded to apply their system to affairs at Washington. It was about this time that, in the course of a debate in the Senate, Marcy gave utterance to the now notorious maxim, "To the victors belong the spoils."

Under Adams the non-partisan character of the public service had been guarded with a scrupulous care that could almost be called exaggerated. Indeed, Adams certainly went altogether too far in his non-partisanship when it came to appointing cabinet and other high officers, his views on such points being not only fantastic, but absolutely wrong. The colorless character of his administration was largely due to his having, in his anxiety to avoid blind and unreasoning adherence to party, committed the only less serious fault of paying too little heed to party; for a healthy party spirit is prerequisite to the performance of effective work in American political life. Adams was not elected purely for himself, but also on account of the men and the principles that he was supposed to represent; and when he partly surrounded himself with men of opposite principles, he just so far, though from the best of motives, betrayed his supporters, and rightly forfeited much of their confidence. But, under him, every public servant felt that, so long as he faithfully served the state, his position was secure, no matter what his political opinions might be.

With the incoming of the Jacksonians all this changed, and terribly for the worse. A perfect reign of terror ensued among the office-holders. In the first month of the new administration more removals took place than during all the previous administrations put together. Appointments were made with little or no attention to fitness, or even honesty, but solely because of personal or political services. Removals were not made in accordance with any known rule at all; the most frivolous pretexts were sufficient, if advanced by useful politicians who needed places already held by capable incumbents. Spying and tale-bearing became prominent features of official life, the meaner office-holders trying to save their own heads by denouncing others. The very best men were unceremoniously and causelessly dismissed; gray-headed clerks, who had been appointed by the earlier presidents,—by Washington, the elder Adams, and Jefferson,—being turned off at an hour's notice, although a quarter of a century's faithful work in the public service had unfitted them to earn their living elsewhere. Indeed, it was upon the best and most efficient men that the blow fell heaviest; the spies, tale-bearers, and tricksters often retained their positions. In 1829 the public service was, as it always had been, administered purely in the interest of the people; and the man who was styled the especial champion of the people dealt that service the heaviest blow it has ever received.

Benton himself always took a sound stand on the civil service question, although his partisanship led him at times to defend Jackson's course when he must have known well that it was indefensible. He viewed with the greatest alarm and hostility the growth of the "spoils system," and early introduced, as chairman of a special committee, a bill to repeal the harmful four years' limitation act. In discussing this proposed bill afterwards, he wrote, in words that apply as much at this time as they did then: "The expiration of the four years' term came to be considered as the termination and vacation of all the offices on which it fell, and the creation of vacancies to be filled at the option of the president. The bill to remedy this defect gave legal effect to the original intention of the law by confining the vacation of office to actual defaulters. The power of the president to dismiss civil officers was not attempted to be curtailed, but the restraints of responsibility were placed upon its exercise by requiring the cause of dismission to be communicated to Congress in each case. The section of the bill to that effect was in these words: *That in all nominations made by the president to the Senate, to fill vacancies occasioned by an exercise of the president's power to remove from office, the fact of the removal shall be stated to the Senate at the same time that the nomination is made, with a statement of the reasons for which such officer may have been removed.* This was intended to operate as a restraint upon removals without cause."

In the "Thirty Years' View" he again writes, in language which would be appropriate from every advanced civil service reformer of the present day, that is, from every disinterested man who has studied the workings of the "spoils system" with any intelligence:—

> I consider "sweeping" removals, as now practiced by both parties, a great political evil in our country, injurious to individuals, to the public service, to the purity of elections, and to the harmony and union of the people. Certainly no individual has a right to an office; no one has an estate or property in a public employment; but when a mere ministerial worker in a subordinate station has learned its duties by experience and approved his fidelity by his conduct, it is an injury to the public service to exchange him for a novice whose only title to the place may be a political badge or partisan service. It is exchanging experience for inexperience, tried ability for untried, and destroying the incentive to good conduct by destroying its reward. To the party displaced it is an injury, he having become a proficient

in that business, expecting to remain in it during good behavior, and finding it difficult, at an advanced age, and with fixed habits, to begin a new career in some new walk of life. It converts elections into scrambles for office, and degrades the government into an office for rewards and punishments; and divides the people of the Union into two adverse parties, each in its turn, and as it becomes dominant, to strip and proscribe the other.

Benton had now taken the position which he was for many years to hold, as the recognized senatorial leader of a great and well-defined party. Until 1828 the prominent political chiefs of the nation had either been its presidents, or had been in the cabinets of these presidents. But after Jackson's time they were in the Senate, and it was on this body that public attention was concentrated. Jackson's cabinet itself showed such a falling off, when compared with the cabinets of any of his predecessors, as to justify the caustic criticism that, when he took office, there came in "the millennium of the minnows." In the Senate, on the contrary, there were never before or since so many men of commanding intellect and powers. Calhoun had been elected as vice-president on the Jacksonian ticket, and was thus, in 1829, presiding over the body of which he soon became an active member; Webster and Clay were already taking their positions as the leaders of the great National Republican, or, as it was afterwards called, Whig party.

When the rupture between Calhoun and the Jacksonian Democrats, and the resignation of the former from the vice-presidency took place, three parties developed in the United States Senate. One was composed of the Jacksonian Democrats, with Benton at their head; one was made up of the little band of Nullifiers, led by Calhoun; and the third included the rather loose array of the Whigs, under Clay and Webster. The feeling of the Jacksonians towards Calhoun and the Nullifiers and towards Clay and the Clay Whigs were largely those of personal animosity; but they had very little of this sentiment towards Webster and his associates, their differences with them being on questions of party principle, or else proceeding from merely sectional causes.

CHAPTER V.

THE STRUGGLE WITH THE NULLIFIERS.

During both Jackson's presidential terms he and his adherents were engaged in two great struggles; that with the Nullifiers, and that with the Bank. Although these struggles were in part synchronous, it will be easier to discuss each by itself.

The nullification movement in South Carolina, during the latter part of the third and early part of the fourth decades in the present century, had nothing to do, except in the most distant way, with slavery. Its immediate cause was the high tariff; remotely it sprang from the same feelings which produced the Virginia and Kentucky resolutions of 1798.

Certain of the Slave States, including those which raised hemp, indigo, and sugar, were high-tariff states; indeed, it was not till towards the close of the presidency of Monroe that there had been much sectional feeling over the policy of protection. Originally, while we were a purely agricultural and mercantile people, free trade was the only economic policy which occurred to us as possible to be followed, the first tariff bill being passed in 1816. South Carolina then was inclined to favor the system, Calhoun himself supporting the bill, and, his subsequent denials to the contrary notwithstanding, distinctly advocating the policy of protection to native industries; while Massachusetts then and afterwards stoutly opposed its introduction, as hostile to her interests. However, the bill was passed, and Massachusetts had to submit to its operation. After 1816 new tariff laws were enacted about every four years, and soon the coast Slave States, except Louisiana, realized that their working was hurtful to the interests of the planters. New England also changed her attitude; and when the protective tariff bill of 1828 came up, its opponents and supporters were sharply divided by sectional lines. But these lines were not such as would have divided the states on the question of slavery. The Northeast and Northwest alike favored the measure, as also did all the Southern States west of the Alleghanies, and Louisiana. It was therefore passed by an overwhelming vote, against the solid opposition of the belt of Southern coast states stretching from Virginia to Mississippi, and including these two.

The states that felt themselves harmed by the tariff did something more than record their disapproval by the votes of their representatives in Congress. They nearly all, through their legislatures, entered emphatic protests against its adoption, as being most harmful to them and dangerous to the Union; and some accompanied their protests with threats as to what would be done if the obnoxious laws should be enforced. They certainly had grounds for discontent. In 1828 the tariff, whether it benefited the country as a whole or not, unquestionably harmed the South; and in a federal Union it is most unwise to pass laws which shall benefit one part of the community to the hurt of another part, when the latter receives no compensation. The truculent and unyielding attitude of the extreme protectionists was irritating in the extreme; for cooler men than the South Carolinians might well have been exasperated at such an utterance as that of Henry Clay, when he stated that for the sake of the "American system"—by which title he was fond of styling a doctrine already ancient in mediæval times—he would "defy the South, the president and the devil."

On the other hand, both the good and the evil effects of the tariff were greatly exaggerated. Some harm to the planter states was doubtless caused by it; but their falling back, as compared with the North, in the race for prosperity, was doubtless caused much more by the presence of slavery, as Dallas, of Pennsylvania, pointed out in the course of some very temperate and moderate remarks in the Senate. Clay's assertions as to what the tariff had done for the West were equally ill-founded, as Benton showed in a good speech, wherein he described picturesquely enough the industries and general condition of his portion of the country, and asserted with truth that its revived prosperity was due to its own resources, entirely independent of federal aid or legislation. He said: "I do not think we are indebted to the high tariff for our fertile lands and our navigable rivers; and I am certain we are indebted to these blessings for the prosperity we enjoy." "In all that comes from the soil the people of the West are rich. They have an abundant supply of food for man and beast, and a large surplus to send abroad. They have the comfortable living which industry creates for itself in a rich soil, but beyond this they are poor.... They have no roads paved or macadamized; no canals or aqueducts; no bridges of stone across the innumerable streams; no edifices dedicated to eternity; no schools for the fine arts; not a public library for which an ordinary scholar would not apologize." Then he went on to speak of the commerce of the West and its exports, "the marching myriads of living animals annually taking their departure from the heart of the West, defiling through the gorges of the Cumberland, the Alleghany, and the Appalachian mountains, or traversing the plains of the South, diverging as they march, ... and the flying steamboats and the fleets of floating arks, loaded with the products of the forest, the farm, and the pasture, following the courses of our noble rivers, and bearing their freights to the great city" of New Orleans.

Unfortunately Benton would interlard even his best speeches with theories of economics often more or less crude, and, still worse, with a series of classic quotations and allusions; for he was grievously afflicted with the rage for cheap pseudo-classicism that Jefferson and his school had borrowed from the French revolutionists. Nor could he resist the temptation to drag in allusions to some favorite hobby. The repeal of the salt-tax was an especial favorite of his. He was perfectly right in attacking the tax, and deserves the greatest credit for the persistency which finally won him the victory. But his associates, unless of a humorous turn of mind, must have found his allusions to it rather tiresome, as when, apropos of the commerce of the Mississippi, and without any possible excuse for speaking of the iniquity of taxing salt, he suddenly alluded to New Orleans as "that great city which revives upon the banks of the Mississippi the name of the greatest of the emperors[2] that ever reigned upon the banks of the Tiber, and who eclipsed the glory of his own heroic exploits by giving an order to his legions never to levy a contribution of salt upon a Roman citizen!"

It must be admitted that the tariff did some harm to the South, and that it was natural for the latter to feel resentment at the way in which it worked. But it must also be remembered that no law can be passed which does not distribute its benefits more or less unequally, and which does not, in all probability, work harm in some cases. Moreover, the South was estopped from complaining of one section being harmed by a law that benefited, or was supposed to benefit, the country at large, by her position in regard to the famous embargo and non-intervention acts. These inflicted infinitely more damage and loss in New England than any tariff law could inflict on South Carolina, and, moreover, were put into execution on account of a quarrel with England forced on by the West and South contrary to the desire of the East. Yet the Southerners were fierce in their denunciations of such of the Federalists as went to the extreme in opposition to them. Even in 1816 Massachusetts had been obliged to submit with good grace to the workings of a tariff which she deemed hostile to her interests, and which many Southerners then advocated. Certainly, even if the new tariff laws were ill-advised, unjust, and unequal in their working, yet they did not, in the most remote degree, justify any effort to break up the Union; especially the South had no business to complain when she herself had joined in laying heavier burdens on the shoulders of New England.

Complain she did, however; and soon added threats to complaints, and was evidently ready to add acts to threats. Georgia, at first, took the lead in denunciation; but South Carolina soon surpassed her, and finally went to the length of advocating and preparing for separation from the Union; a step that produced a revulsion of feeling even among her fellow anti-tariff states. The South Carolinian statesmen now proclaimed the doctrine of nullification,—that is, proclaimed that if any state deemed a federal law improper, it could proceed to declare that law null and void so far as its own territory was concerned,—and, as a corollary, that it had the right forcibly to prevent execution of this void law within its borders. This was proclaimed, not as an exercise of the right of revolution, which, in the last resort, belongs, of course, to every community and class, but as a constitutional privilege.

Jefferson was quoted as the father of the idea, and the Kentucky resolutions of 1798-99, which he drew, were cited as the precedent for the South Carolinian action. In both these last assertions the Nullifiers were correct. Jefferson was the father of nullification, and therefore of secession. He used the word "nullify" in the original draft which he supplied to the Kentucky legislature, and though that body struck it out of the resolutions which they passed in 1798, they inserted it in those of the following year. This was done mainly as an unscrupulous party move on Jefferson's part, and when his side came into power he became a firm upholder of the Union; and, being constitutionally unable to put a proper value on truthfulness, he even denied that his resolutions could be construed to favor nullification—though they could by no possibility be construed to mean anything else.

At this time it is not necessary to discuss nullification as a constitutional dogma; it is an absurdity too great to demand serious refutation. The United States has the same right to protect itself from death by nullification, secession, or rebellion, that a man has to protect himself from death by assassination. Calhoun's hair-splitting and metaphysical disquisitions on the constitutionality of nullification have now little more practical interest than have the extraordinary arguments and discussions of the school-men of the Middle Ages.

But at the time they were of vital interest, for they were words which it was known South Carolina was prepared to back up by deeds. Calhoun was vice-president, the second officer in the federal government, and yet also the avowed leader of the most bitter disunionists. His state supported him by an overwhelming majority, although even within its own borders there was an able opposition, headed by the gallant and loyal family of the Draytons,— the same family that afterwards furnished the captain of Farragut's flag-ship, the glorious old Hartford. There was a strong sentiment in the other Southern States in his favor; the public men of South Carolina made speech after speech goading him on to take even more advanced ground.

In Washington the current at first seemed to be all setting in favor of the Nullifiers; they even counted on Jackson's support, as he was a Southerner and a states'-rights man. But he was also a strong Unionist, and, moreover, at this time, felt very bitterly towards Calhoun, with whom he had just had a split, and had in consequence remodeled his cabinet, thrusting out all Calhoun's supporters, and adopting Van Buren as his political heir,—the position which it was hitherto supposed the great Carolina separatist occupied.

The first man to take up the gauntlet the Nullifiers had thrown down was Webster, in his famous reply to Hayne. He, of course, voiced the sentiment of the Whigs, and especially of the Northeast, where the high tariff was regarded with peculiar favor, where the Union feeling was strong, and where there was a certain antagonism felt towards the South. The Jacksonian Democrats, whose strength lay in the West, had not yet spoken. They were, for the most part, neither ultra protectionists nor absolute free-traders; Jackson's early presidential utterances had given offense to the South by not condemning all high-tariff legislation, but at the same time had declared in favor of a much more moderate degree of protection than suited the Whigs. Only a few weeks after Webster's speech Jackson's chance came, and he declared himself in unmistakable terms. It was on the occasion of the Jefferson birthday banquet, April 13, 1830. An effort was then being made to have Jefferson's birthday celebrated annually; and the Nullifiers, rightly claiming him as their first and chief apostle, attempted to turn this particular feast into a demonstration in favor of nullification. Most of the speakers present were actively or passively in favor of the movement, and the toasts proposed strongly savored of the new doctrine. But Jackson, Benton, and a number of other Union men were in attendance also, and when it came to Jackson's turn he electrified the audience by proposing: "Our federal Union; it must be preserved." Calhoun at once answered with: "The Union; next to our liberty the most dear; may we all remember that it can only be preserved by respecting the rights of the states and distributing equally the benefit and burden of the Union." The issue between the president and the vice-president was now complete, and the Jacksonian Democracy was squarely committed against nullification. Jackson had risen to the occasion as only a strong and a great man could rise, and his few, telling words, finely contrasting at every point with Calhoun's utterances, rang throughout the whole country, and will last as long as our government. One result, at least, the Nullifiers accomplished,—they completely put an end to the Jefferson birthday celebrations.

The South Carolinians had no intention of flinching from the contest which they had provoked, even when they saw that the North and West were united against them, and though the tide began to set the same way in their sister states of the South; North Carolina, among the latter, being the first and most pronounced in her support of the president and denunciation of the Nullifiers. The men of the Palmetto State have always ranked high for hotheaded courage, and they soon showed that they had wills as fiery as that of Jackson himself. Yet in the latter they had met an antagonist well worthy of any foeman's steel. In declining an invitation to be present at Charleston, on July 4, 1831, the president again defined most clearly his position in favor of the Union, and his words had an especial significance because he let it be seen that he was fully determined to back them up by force if necessary. But his letter only had the effect of inflaming still more the minds of the South Carolinians. The prime cause of irritation, the tariff, still remained; and in 1832, Clay, having entered the Senate after a long retirement from politics, put the finishing stroke to their anger by procuring the passage of a new tariff bill, which left the planter states almost as badly off as did the law of 1828. Jackson signed this, although not believing that it went far enough in the reduction of duties.

In the presidential election of 1832, Jackson defeated Clay by an enormous majority; Van Buren was elected vice-president, there being thus a Northern man on the ticket. South Carolina declined to take part in the election, throwing away her vote. Again, it must be kept in mind that the slave question did not shape, or, indeed, enter into this contest at all, directly, although beginning to be present in the background as a source of irritation. In 1832 there was ten-fold more feeling in the North against Masonry, and secret societies generally, than there was against slavery.

Benton threw himself in, heart and soul, with the Union party, acting as Jackson's right-hand man throughout the contest with South Carolina, and showing an even more resolute and unflinching front than Old Hickory himself. No better or trustier ally than the Missouri statesman, in a hard fight for a principle, could be desired. He was intensely national in all his habits of thought; he took a deep, personal pride in all his country,—North, South, East, and West. He had been very loath to believe that any movement hostile to the Union was really on foot; but once thoroughly convinced of it he chose his own line of action without an instant's hesitation.

A fortnight after the presidential election South Carolina passed her ordinance of nullification, directed against the tariff laws generally, and against those of 1828 and 1832 in particular. The ordinance was to take effect on February 1st; and if meantime the federal government should make any attempt to enforce the laws, the fact of such attempt was to end the continuance of South Carolina in the Union.

Jackson promptly issued a proclamation against nullification, composed jointly by himself and the great Louisiana jurist and statesman, Livingston. It is one of the ablest, as well as one of the most important, of all American state papers. It is hard to see how any American can read it now without feeling his veins thrill. Some claim it as being mainly the work of Jackson, others as that of Livingston; it is great honor for either to have had a hand in its production.

In his annual message the president merely referred, in passing, to the Nullifiers, expressing his opinion that the action in reducing the duties, which the extinction of the public debt would permit and require, would put an end to the proceedings. As matters grew more threatening, however, South Carolina making every preparation for war and apparently not being conciliated in the least by the evident desire in Congress to meet her more than half-way on the tariff question, Jackson sent a special message to both houses. He had already sent General Scott to Charleston, and had begun the concentration of certain military and naval forces in or near the state boundaries. He now asked Congress to pass a measure to enable him to deal better with possible resistance to the laws. South Carolina having complained of the oppressed condition in which she found herself, owing to the working of the tariff, Jackson, in his message, with some humor, quoted in reply the last Thanksgiving proclamation of her governor, wherein he dilated upon the state's unexampled prosperity and happiness.

It must always be kept in mind in describing the attitude of the Jacksonian Democrats towards the Nullifiers that they were all along, especially in the West, hostile to a very high tariff. Jackson and Benton had always favored a much lower tariff than that established in 1828 and hardly changed in 1832. It was no change of front on their part now to advocate a reduction of duties. Jackson and Benton both felt that there was much ground for South Carolina's original complaint, although as strongly opposed to her nullification attitude as any Northerner. Most of the Southern senators and representatives, though opposed to nullification, were almost equally hostile to the high tariff; and very many others were at heart in sympathy with nullification itself. The intensely national and anti-separatist tone of Jackson's declaration,—a document that might well have come from Washington or Lincoln, and that would have reflected high honor on either,—though warmly approved by Benton, was very repugnant to many of the Southern Democrats, and was too much even for certain of the Whigs. In fact, it reads like the utterance of some great Federalist or Republican leader. The feeling in Congress, as a whole, was as strong against the tariff as it was against nullification; and Jackson had to take this into account, all the more because not only was he in some degree of the same way of thinking, but also many of his followers entertained the sentiment even more earnestly.

Calhoun introduced a series of nullification resolutions into the Senate, and defended them strongly in the prolonged constitutional debate that followed. South Carolina meanwhile put off the date at which her decrees were to take effect, so that she might see what Congress would do. Beyond question, Jackson's firmness, and the way in which he was backed up by Benton, Webster, and their followers, was having some effect. He had openly avowed his intention, if matters went too far, of hanging Calhoun "higher than Haman." He unquestionably meant to imprison him, as well as the other South Carolina leaders, the instant that state came into actual collision with the Union; and to the end of his life regretted, and with reason, that he had not done so without waiting for an overt act of resistance. Some historians have treated this as if it were an idle threat; but such it certainly was not. Jackson undoubtedly fully meant what he said, and would have acted promptly had the provocation occurred, and, moreover, he would have been sustained by the country. He was not the man to weigh minutely what would and what would not fall just on one side or the other of the line defining treason; nor was it the time for too scrupulous adherence to precise wording. Had a collision occurred, neither Calhoun nor his colleague would ever have been permitted to leave Washington; and brave though they were, the fact unquestionably had much influence with them.

Webster was now acting heartily with Benton. He introduced a set of resolutions which showed that in the matters both of the tariff and of nullification his position was much the same as was that of the Missourian. Unfortunately Congress, as a whole, was by no means so stiff-kneed. A certain number of Whigs followed Webster, and a certain number of Democrats clung to Benton; but most Southerners were very reluctant to allow pressure to be brought to bear on South Carolina, and many Northerners were as willing to compromise as Henry Clay himself. In accordance with Jackson's recommendations two bills were introduced: one the so-called "Force bill," to allow the president to take steps to defend the federal authority in the event of actual collision; and the other a moderate, and, on the whole, proper tariff bill, to reduce protective duties. Both were introduced by administration supporters. Benton and Webster warmly sustained the "Force bill," which was bitterly attacked by the Nullifiers and by most of the Southerners, who really hardly knew what stand to take, the leading opponent being Tyler of Virginia, whose disunion attitude was almost as clearly marked as that of Calhoun himself. The measure was eminently just, and was precisely what the crisis demanded; and the Senate finally passed it and sent it to the House.

All this time an obstinate struggle was going on over the tariff bill. Calhoun and his sympathizers were beginning to see that there was real danger ahead, alike to themselves, their constituents, and their principles, if they followed unswervingly the course they had laid down; and the weak-kneed brethren on the other side, headed by Clay, were becoming even more uneasy. Calhoun wished to avert collision with the federal government; Clay was quite as anxious to avoid an outbreak in the South and to save what he could of the protective system, which was evidently doomed. Calhoun was willing to sacrifice some of his constitutional theories in regard to protection; Clay was ready greatly to reduce protection itself. Each, of them, but especially Clay, was prepared to shift his stand somewhat from that of abstract moral right to that of expediency. Benton and Webster were too resolute and determined in their hostility to any form of yielding to South Carolina's insolent defiance to admit any hope of getting them to accept a compromise; but the majority of the members were known to be only too ready to jump at any half-way measure which would patch up the affair for the present, no matter what the sacrifice of principle or how great the risk incurred for the future. Accordingly, Clay and Calhoun met and agreed on a curious bill, in reality recognizing the protective system, but making a great although gradual reduction of duties; and Clay introduced this as a "compromise measure." It was substituted in the House for the administration tariff bill, was passed and sent to the Senate. It gave South Carolina much, but not all, that she demanded. Her representatives announced themselves satisfied, and supported it, together with all their Southern sympathizers. Webster and Benton fought it stoutly to the last, but it was passed by a great majority; a few Northerners followed Webster, and Benton received fair support from his Missouri colleagues and the Maryland senators; the other senators, Whigs and Democrats alike, voted for the measure. Many of the Southerners were imbued with separatist principles, although not yet to the extent that Calhoun was; others, though Union men, did not possess the unflinching will and stern strength of character that enabled Benton to stand out against any section of the country, even his own, if it was wrong. Silas Wright, of New York, a typical Northern "dough-face" politician, gave exact expression to the "dough-face" sentiment, which induced Northern members to vote for the compromise, when he stated that he was unalterably opposed to the principle of the bill, but that on account of the attitude of South Carolina, and of the extreme desire which he had to remove all cause of discontent in that state, and in order to enable her again to become an affectionate member of the Union, he would vote for what was satisfactory to her, although repugnant to himself. Wright, Marcy, and their successors in New York politics, almost up to the present day, certainly carried cringing subserviency to the South to a pitch that was fairly sublime.

The "Force bill" and the compromise tariff bill passed both houses nearly simultaneously, and were sent up to the president, who signed both on the same day. His signing the compromise bill was a piece of weakness out of keeping with his whole character, and especially out of keeping with his previous course towards the Nullifiers. The position assumed by Benton and Webster, that South Carolina should be made to submit first and should have the justice of her claims examined into afterwards, was unquestionably the only proper attitude.

Benton wrote:—

> My objections to this bill, and to its mode of being passed, were deep and abiding, and went far beyond its own obnoxious provisions, and all the transient and temporary considerations connected with it.... A compromise made with a state in arms is a capitulation to that state.... The injury was great then, and a permanent evil example. It remitted the government to the condition of the old confederation, acting upon sovereignties instead of

individuals. It violated the feature of our Union which discriminated it from all confederacies that ever existed, and which was wisely and patriotically put into the Constitution to save it from the fate which had attended all confederacies, ancient and modern.... The framers of our Constitution established a Union instead of a League—to be sovereign and independent within its sphere, acting upon persons through its own laws and courts, instead of acting on communities through persuasion or force. The effect of this compromise legislation was to destroy this great feature of our Union—to bring the general and state governments into conflict—and to substitute a sovereign state for an offending individual as often as a state chose to make the cause of that individual her own.

Not only was Benton's interpretation of the Constitution sound, and one that by the course of events has now come to be universally accepted, but his criticisms on the wisdom of the compromise bill were perfectly just. Had the Anti-Nullifiers stood firm, the Nullifiers would probably have given way, and if not, would certainly have been crushed. Against a solid North and West, with a divided South, even her own people not being unanimous, and with Jackson as chief executive, South Carolina could not have made even a respectable resistance. A salutary lesson then might very possibly have saved infinite trouble and bloodshed thereafter. But in Jackson's case it must be remembered that, so far as his acts depended purely upon his own will and judgment, no fault can be found with him; he erred only in ratifying a compromise agreed to by the vast majority of the representatives of the people in both houses of Congress.

The battle did not result in a decisive victory for either side. This was shown by the very fact that each party insisted that it had won a signal triumph. Calhoun and Clay afterwards quarreled in the senate chamber as to which had given up the more in the compromise. South Carolina had declared, first, that the tariff was unconstitutional, and therefore to be opposed upon principle; second, that it worked injustice to her interests, and must be abolished forthwith; thirdly, that, if it were not so abolished, she would assert her power to nullify a federal law, and, if necessary, would secede from the Union. When her representatives agreed to the compromise bill, they abandoned the first point; the second was decided largely in her favor, though protection was not by any means entirely given up; the third she was allowed to insist upon with impunity, although the other side, by passing the "Force bill," showed that in case matters did proceed to extremities they were prepared to act upon the opposite conviction. Still, she gained most of that for which she contended, and the victory, as a whole, rested with her.

Calhoun's purposes seem to have been, in the main, pure; but few criminals have worked as much harm to their country as he did. The plea of good intentions is not one that can be allowed to have much weight in passing historical judgment upon a man whose wrong-headedness and distorted way of looking at things produced, or helped to produce, such incalculable evil; there is a wide political applicability in the remark attributed to a famous Texan, to the effect that he might, in the end, pardon a man who shot him on purpose, but that he would surely never forgive one who did so accidentally.

Without doubt, the honors of the nullification dispute were borne off by Benton and Webster. The latter's reply to Hayne is, perhaps, the greatest single speech of the nineteenth century, and he deserves the highest credit for the stubbornness with which he stood by his colors to the last. There never was any question of Webster's courage; on the occasions when he changed front he was actuated by self-interest and ambition, not by timidity. Usually he appears as an advocate rather than an earnest believer in the cause he represents; but when it came to be a question of the Union, he felt what he said with the whole strength of his nature.

An even greater meed of praise attaches to Benton for the unswerving fidelity which he showed to the Union in this crisis. Webster was a high-tariff man, and was backed up by all the sectional antipathies of the Northeast in his opposition to the Nullifiers; Benton, on the contrary, was a believer in a low tariff, or in one for revenue merely, and his sectional antipathies were the other way. Yet, even when deserted by his chief, and when he was opposed to every senator from south of the Potomac and the Ohio, he did not flinch for a moment from his attitude of aggressive loyalty to the national Union. He had a singularly strong and upright character; this country has never had a statesman more fearlessly true to his convictions, when great questions were at stake, no matter what might be the cost to himself, or the pressure from outside,—even when, as happened later, his own state was against him. Intellectually he cannot for a moment be compared to the great Massachusetts senator; but morally he towers much higher.

Yet, while praising Jackson and Benton for their behavior towards South Carolina, we cannot forget that but a couple of years previously they had not raised their voices even in the mildest rebuke of Georgia for conduct which, though not nearly so bad in degree as that of South Carolina, was of much the same kind. Towards the close of Adams's term, Georgia had bid defiance to the mandates of the Supreme Court, and proceeded to settle the Indian question within her borders without regard to the authority of the United States, and these matters were still unsettled when Jackson became president. Unfortunately he let his personal feelings bias him; and, as he took the Western and Georgian view of the Indian question, and, moreover, hated the

Supreme Court because it was largely Federalist in its composition, he declined to interfere. David Crockett, himself a Union man and a nationalist to the backbone, rated Jackson savagely, and with justice, for the inconsistency of his conduct in the two cases, accusing him of having, by his harmful leniency to Georgia, encouraged South Carolina to act as she did, and ridiculing him because, while he smiled at the deeds of the one state, when the like acts were done by the other, "he took up the rod of correction and shook it over her".

CHAPTER VI.

JACKSON AND BENTON MAKE WAR ON THE BANK.

If the struggle with the Nullifiers showed Benton at his best, in the conflict with the Bank he exhibited certain qualities which hardly place him in so favorable a light. Jackson's attack upon the Bank was a move undertaken mainly on his own responsibility, and one which, at first, most of his prominent friends were alarmed to see him undertake. Benton alone supported him from the beginning. Captain and lieutenant alike intensely appreciated the joy of battle; they cared for a fight because it was a fight, and the certainty of a struggle, such as would have daunted weaker or more timid men, simply offered to them an additional inducement to follow out the course they had planned. Benton's thorough-going support was invaluable to Jackson. The president sorely needed a friend in the Senate who would uphold him through thick and thin, and who yet commanded the respect of all his opponents by his strength, ability, and courage. To be sure, Benton's knowledge of financial economics was not always profound; but, on the other hand, a thorough mastery of the laws of finance would have been, in this fight, a very serious disadvantage to any champion of Jackson.

The rights and wrongs of this matter have been worn threadbare in countless discussions. For much of the hostility of Jackson and Benton towards the Bank, there were excellent grounds; but many of their actions were wholly indefensible and very harmful in their results to the country. An assault upon what Benton called "the money power" is apt to be popular in a democratic republic, partly on account of the vague fear with which the poorer and more ignorant voters regard a powerful institution, whose working they do not understand, and partly on account of the jealousy they feel towards those who are better off than themselves. When these feelings are appealed to by men who are intensely in earnest, and who are themselves convinced of the justice and wisdom of their course, they become very formidable factors in any political contest.

The struggle first became important when the question of the re-charter of the Bank was raised, towards the end of Jackson's first term, the present charter still having three years to run. This charter had in it many grave faults; and there might well be a question as to whether it should be renewed. The Bank itself, beyond doubt, possessed enormous power; too much power for its own or outsiders' good. Its president, Biddle, was a man of some ability, but conceited to the last degree, untruthful, and to a certain extent unscrupulous in the use he made of the political influence of the great moneyed institution over which he presided. Some of the financial theories on which he managed the Bank were wrong; yet, on the whole, it was well conducted, and under its care the monetary condition of the country was quiet and good, infinitely better than it had been before, or than, under the auspices of the Jacksonian Democracy, it afterwards became.

The two great reasons for Jackson's success throughout his political career were to be found in the strength of the feeling in his favor among the poorer and least educated classes of voters, and in the ardent support given him by the low politicians, who, by playing on his prejudices and passions, moulded him to their wishes, and who organized and perfected in their own and his interests a great political machine, founded on the "spoils system"; and both the Jacksonian rank and file and the Jacksonian politicians soon agreed heartily in their opposition to the Bank. Jackson and Benton opposed it for the same reasons that the bulk of their followers did; that is to say, partly from honest and ignorant prejudice and partly from a well-founded feeling of distrust as to some of its actions. The mass of their fellow party-leaders and henchmen assailed it with the cry that it was exerting its influence to debauch politics, while at the same time they really sought to use it as a power in politics on their own side.

Jackson, in his first annual message in 1829, had hinted that he was opposed to the re-charter of the Bank, then a question of the future and not to arise for four or five years. At the same time he had called in question the constitutionality and expediency of the Bank's existence, and had criticised as vicious its currency system. The matter of constitutionality had been already decided by the Supreme Court, the proper tribunal, and was, and had been for years, an accepted fact; it was an absurdity to call it in question. As regards the matter of expediency, certainly the Jacksonians failed signally to put anything better in its place. Yet it was undeniable that there were grave defects in the currency system.

The president's message roused but little interest, and what little it did rouse was among the Bank's friends. At once these began to prepare the way for the re-charter by an active and extensive agitation in its favor. The main bank was at Philadelphia, but it had branches everywhere, and naturally each branch bank was a centre of opposition to the president's proposed policy. As the friends of the Bank were greatly interested, and as the matter did not immediately concern those who afterwards became its foes, the former, for the time, had it all their own way, and the drift of public opinion seemed to be strongly in its favor.

Benton was almost the only public man of prominence who tried to stem this tide from the beginning. Jackson's own party associates were originally largely against him, and so he stood all the more in need of the vigorous support which he received from the Missouri senator. Indeed, it would be unfair in the matter of the attack on the Bank to call Benton Jackson's follower; he might with more propriety be called the leader in the assault, although of course he could accomplish little compared with what was done by the great popular idol. He had always been hostile to the Bank, largely as a matter of Jeffersonian tradition, and he had shown his hostility by resolutions introduced in the Senate before Jackson was elected president.

Early in 1831 he asked leave to introduce a resolution against the re-charter of the Bank; his purpose being merely to give formal notice of war against it, and to attempt to stir up a current of feeling counter to that which then seemed to be generally prevailing in its favor. In his speech he carefully avoided laying stress upon any such abstract point as that of constitutionality, and dwelt instead upon the questions that would affect the popular mind; assailing the Bank "as having too much power over the people and the government, over business and politics, and as too much disposed to exercise that power to the prejudice of the freedom and equality which should prevail in a republic, to be allowed to exist in our country." The force of such an argument in a popular election will be acknowledged by all practical politicians. But, although Benton probably believed what he said, or at any rate most of it, he certainly ought not to have opened the discussion of a great financial measure with a demagogic appeal to caste prejudices. He wished to substitute a gold currency in the place of the existing bank-notes, and was not disturbed at all as to how he would supply the place of the Bank, saying: "I am willing to see the charter expire, without providing any substitute for the present Bank. I am willing to see the currency of the federal government left to the hard money mentioned and intended in the Constitution; ... every species of paper might be left to the state authorities, unrecognized by the federal government!" Of the beauties of such a system as the last the country later on received practical demonstration. Some of his utterances, however, could be commended to the friends of greenbacks and of dishonest money even at the present day, as when he says: "Gold and silver are the best currency for a republic; it suits the men of middle property and the working people best; and if I was going to establish a workingman's party it should be on the basis of hard money—a hard-money party against a paper party." The Bank was in Philadelphia; much of the stock was held in the East, and a good deal was held abroad, which gave Benton a chance to play on sectional feelings, as follows: "To whom is all the power granted? To a company of private individuals, many of them foreigners, and the mass of them residing in a remote and narrow corner of the Union, unconnected by any sympathy with the fertile regions of the Great Valley, in which the natural power of this Union—the power of numbers—will be found to reside long before the renewed term of a second charter would expire." Among the other sentences occurs the following bit of pure demagogic pyrotechnics: "It [the Bank] tends to aggravate the inequality of fortunes; to make the rich richer and the poor poorer; to multiply nabobs and paupers; and to deepen and widen the gulf which separates Dives from Lazarus. A great moneyed power is favorable to great capitalists, for it is the principle of money to favor money. It is unfavorable to small capitalists, for it is the principle of money to eschew the needy and unfortunate. It is injurious to the laboring classes." Altogether it was not a speech to be proud of. The Senate refused permission to introduce the resolution by the close vote of twenty-three to twenty.

Benton lived only a generation after that one which had itself experienced oppression from a king, from an aristocratic legislature and from a foreign power; and so his rant about the undue influence of foreigners in our governmental affairs, and his declamation over the purely supposititious powers that were presumed to be conspiring against the welfare of the poorer classes probably more nearly expressed his real feelings than would be the case with the similar utterances of any leading statesman nowadays. He was an enthusiastic believer in the extreme Jeffersonian doctrinaire views as to the will of the majority being always right, and as to the moral perfection of the average voter. Like his fellow-statesmen he failed to see the curious absurdity of supporting black slavery, and yet claiming universal suffrage for whites as a divine right, not as a mere matter of expediency resulting on the whole better than any other method. He had not learned that the majority in a democracy has no more right to tyrannize over a minority than, under a different system, the latter would have to oppress the former; and that, if there is a moral principle at stake, the saying that the voice of the people is the voice of God may be quite as untrue, and do quite as much mischief, as the old theory of the divine right of kings. The distinguishing feature of our American governmental system is the freedom of the individual; it is quite as important to prevent his being oppressed by many men as it is to save him from the tyranny of one.

This speech on the re-charter showed a great deal of wide reading and much information; but a good part of it was sheer declamation, in the turgid, pompous style that Benton, as well as a great many other American public speakers, was apt to mistake for genuine oratory. His subsequent speech on the currency, however, was much better. This was likewise delivered on the occasion of asking leave to present a joint resolution, which leave was refused. The branch draft system was the object of the assault. These branch drafts were for even sums of small denomination, circulating like bank-notes; they were drawn on the parent bank at Philadelphia to the order of some officer of the branch bank and were indorsed by the latter to bearer. Thus paper was issued at one place which was payable at another and a distant place; and among other results there ensued a constant inflation of credit. They were very mischievous in their workings; they had none of the marks of convertible bank-notes or money, and so long as credit was active there could be no check on the inflation of the currency by them. Payment could be voluntarily made at the branch banks whence issued, but if it was refused the owner had only the right to go to Philadelphia and sue the directors there. Most of these drafts were issued at the most remote and inaccessible branches, the payment of them being, therefore, much delayed by distance and difficulty; nor were the directors liable for excessive issues. They constituted the bulk of all the paper seen in circulation; they were supposed to be equivalent to money, but being bills of exchange they were merely negotiable instruments; they did not have the properties of bank-notes, which are constantly and directly interchangeable with money. In their issue Biddle had laid himself open to attack; and in defending them he certainly did not always speak the truth, willfully concealing or coloring facts. Moreover, his self-satisfaction and the foolish pride in his own power, which he could not conceal, led him into making imprudent boasts as to the great power the Bank could exercise over other local banks, and over the general prosperity of the country, while dilating upon its good conduct in not using this power to the disadvantage of the public. All this was playing into Benton's hands. He showed some of the evils of the branch draft system, although apparently not seeing others that were quite as important. He attacked the Bank for some real and many imaginary wrongdoings; and quoted Biddle himself as an authority for the existence of powers dangerous to the welfare of the state.

The advocates of the Bank were still in the majority in both houses of Congress, and soon began preparations for pushing through a bill for the recharter. The issue began to become political. Webster, Clay, and most of the other anti-administration men were for the Bank; and so when the convention of the National Republicans, who soon afterwards definitely assumed the name of Whigs, took place, they declared heartily in its favor, and nominated for the presidency its most enthusiastic supporter, Henry Clay. The Bank itself unquestionably preferred not to be dragged into politics; but Clay, thinking he saw a chance for a successful stroke, fastened upon it, and the convention that nominated him made the fight against Jackson on the ground that he was hostile to the Bank. Even had this not already been the case no more certain method of insuring his hostility could have been adopted.

Still, however, many of Jackson's supporters were also advocates of recharter; and the bill for that purpose commanded the majority in Congress. Benton took the lead in organizing the opposition, not with the hope of preventing its passage, but "to attack incessantly, assail at all points, display the evil of the institution, rouse the people, and prepare them to sustain the veto." In other words, he was preparing for an appeal to the people, and working to secure an anti-Bank majority in the next Congress. He instigated and prepared the investigation into the affairs of the Bank, which was made in the House, and he led the harassing parliamentary warfare carried on against the re-chartering bill in the Senate. He himself seems to have superintended the preparation of the charges which were investigated by the House. A great flurry was made over them, Benton and all his friends claiming that they were fully substantiated; but the only real point scored was that against the branch drafts. Benton, with the majority of the committee of investigation, had the loosest ideas as to what a bank ought to do, loud though they were in denunciation of what this particular Bank was alleged to have done.

Webster made the great argument in favor of the re-charter bill. Benton took the lead in opposition, stating, what was probably true,—that the bill was brought up so long before the charter expired for political reasons, and criticising it as premature; a criticism unfortunately applicable with even greater force to Jackson's message. His speech was largely mere talking against time, and he wandered widely from the subject. Among other things he invoked the aid of the principle of states'-rights, because the Bank then had power to establish branches in any state, whether the latter liked it or not, and free from state taxation. He also appealed to the Western members as such, insisting that the Bank discriminated against their section of the country in favor of the East; the facts being that the shrewdness and commercial morality of the Northeast, particularly of New England, saved them from the evils brought on the Westerners by the foolishness with which they abused their credit and the laxness with which they looked on monetary obligations. But in spite of all that Benton could do the bill passed both houses, the Senate voting in its favor by twenty-eight ayes against twenty nays.

Jackson, who never feared anything, and was more than ready to accept the fight which was in some measure forced on him, yet which in some degree he had courted, promptly vetoed the bill in a message which stated some truths forcibly and fearlessly, which developed some very queer constitutional and financial theories, and which contained a number of absurdities, evidently put in, not for the benefit of the Senate, but to influence voters at the coming presidential election. The leaders of the opposition felt obliged to make a show of trying to pass the bill over the veto in order to get a chance to answer Jackson. Webster again opened the argument. Clay made the fiercest onslaught, assailing the president personally, besides attacking the veto power, and trying to discredit its use. But the presidential power of veto is among the best features of our government, and Benton had no difficulty in making a good defense of it; although many of the arguments adduced by him in its favor were entirely unsound, being based on the wholly groundless assumption that the function of the president corresponded to that of the ancient Roman tribune of the people, and was supposed to be exercised in the interests of the people to control the legislature—thus willfully overlooking the fact that the legislature also was elected by the people. When on his ultra-democratic hobby Benton always rode very loose in the saddle, and with little knowledge of where he was going. Clay and Benton alike drew all sorts of analogies between the state of affairs in the United States and that formerly prevailing in France, England, and above all in the much-suffering republics of antiquity. Benton insisted that the Bank had wickedly persuaded the West to get in debt to it so as to have that section in its power, and that the Western debt had been created with a view to political engineering; the fact being that the Westerners had run into debt purely by their own fault, and that the Bank itself was seriously alarmed at the condition of its Western branches. The currency being in much worse shape in the West than in the Northeast, gold and silver naturally moved towards the latter place; and this result of their own shortcomings was again held up as a grievance of the Westerners against the Bank. He also read a severe lecture on the interests of party discipline to the Democrats who had voted for the re-charter, assuring them that they could not continue to be both for the Bank and for Jackson. The Jacksonian Democracy, nominally the party of the multitude, was in reality the nearest approach the United States has ever seen to the "one man power;" and to break with Jackson was to break with the Democratic party. The alternative of expulsion or of turning a somersault being thus plainly presented to the recalcitrant members, they for the most part chose the latter, and performed the required feat of legislative acrobatics with the most unobtrusive and submissive meekness. The debate concluded with a sharp and undignified interchange of personalities between the Missouri and Kentucky senators, Clay giving Benton the lie direct, and the latter retorting in kind. Each side, of course, predicted the utter ruin of the country, if the other prevailed. Benton said that, if the Bank conquered, the result would be the establishment of an oligarchy, and then of a monarchy, and finally the death of the Republic by corruption. Webster stated as his belief that, if the sentiments of the veto message received general approbation, the Constitution could not possibly survive its fiftieth year. Webster, however, in that debate, showed to good advantage. Benton was no match for him, either as a thinker or as a speaker; but with the real leader of the Whig party, Henry Clay, he never had much cause to fear comparison.

All the state banks were of course rabidly in favor of Jackson; and the presidential election of 1832 was largely fought on the bank issue. In Pennsylvania, however, the feeling for the Bank was only less strong than that for Jackson; and accordingly that Bœotian community sapiently cast its electoral votes for the latter, while instructing its senators and representatives to support the former. But the complete and hopeless defeat of Clay by Jackson sealed the fate of the Bank. Jackson was not even content to let it die naturally by the lapse of its charter. His attitude towards it so far had been one for which much could be said; indeed, very good grounds can be shown for thinking his veto proper. But of the impropriety of his next step there could be no possible question. Congress had passed a resolution declaring its belief in the safety of the United States deposits in the Bank; but the president, in the summer of 1833, removed these deposits and placed them in certain state banks. He experienced some difficulty in getting a secretary of the treasury who would take such a step; finally he found one in Taney.

The Bank memorialized Congress at once; and the anti-administration majority in the Senate forthwith took up the quarrel. They first rejected Jackson's nominations for bank directors, and then refused to confirm Taney himself. Two years later Jackson made the latter Chief Justice of the Supreme Court, in which position he lived to do even more mischief than he had time or opportunity to accomplish as secretary of the treasury.

Benton was the administration champion in the Senate. Opposed to him were Webster and Clay, as leaders of the Whigs, supported for the time being by Calhoun. The feeling of Clay and Calhoun against the president was bitterly personal, and was repaid by his rancorous hatred. But Webster, though he was really on most questions even more antagonistic to the ideas of the Jacksonian school, always remained personally on good terms with its leaders.

Clay introduced a resolution directing the return of the deposits; Benton opposed it; it passed by a vote of twenty-eight to eighteen, but was lost in the House. Clay then introduced a resolution demanding to know from the president whether the paper alleged to have been published by his authority as having been read to the cabinet, in relation to the removal of the deposits, was genuine or not; and, if it was, asking for a copy. Benton opposed the motion, which nevertheless passed. But the president refused to accede to the demand. Meanwhile the new departure in banking, inaugurated by the president, was working badly. One of the main grounds for removing the deposits was the allegation that they were used to debauch politics. This was never proved against the old United States Bank; but under Jackson's administration, which corrupted the public service in every way, the deposits became fruitful sources of political reward and bribery.

Clay then introduced his famous resolution censuring the president for his action, and supported it in a long and fiery speech; a speech which, like most of Clay's, was received by his followers at the time with rapture, but in which this generation fails to find the sign of that remarkable ability with which his own contemporaries credited the great Kentuckian. He attacked Jackson with fierce invective, painting him as an unscrupulous tyrant, who was inaugurating a revolution in the government of the Union. But he was outdone by Calhoun, who, with continual interludes of complacent references to the good already done by the Nullifiers, assailed Jackson as one of a band of artful, corrupt, and cunning politicians, and drew a picture even more lurid than Clay's of the future of the country, and the danger of impending revolution. Webster's speeches were more self-contained in tone. Benton was the only Jacksonian senator who could contend with the great Nullifier and the two great Whigs; and he replied at length, and in much the same style as they had spoken.

The Senate was flooded with petitions in favor of the Bank, which were presented with suitable speeches by the leading Whigs. Benton ridiculed the exaggerated tone of alarm in which these petitions were drawn, and declared that the panic, excitement, and suffering existing in business circles throughout the country were due to the deliberate design of the Bank, and afforded a fresh proof that the latter was a dangerous power to the state.

The resolution of censure was at last passed by a vote of twenty-six to twenty, and Jackson, in a fury, sent in a written protest against it, which the Senate refused to receive. The excitement all over the country was intense throughout the struggle. The suffering, which was really caused by the president's act, but which was attributed by his supporters to the machinations of the Bank, was very real; even Benton admitted this, although contending that it was not a natural result of the policy pursued, but had been artificially excited—or, as he very clumsily phrased it, "though fictitious and forged, yet the distress was real, and did an immensity of damage." Neither Jackson nor Benton yielded an inch to the outside pressure; the latter was the soul of the fight in Congress, making over thirty speeches during the struggle.

During the debate on receiving the president's protest, Benton gave notice of his intention at an early day to move to expunge from the journal the resolution of censure. This idea was entirely his own, and he gave the notice without having consulted anybody. It was, however, a motion after Jackson's own heart, as the latter now began to look upon the affair as purely personal to himself. His party accepted this view of the matter with a servile alacrity only surpassed by the way in which its leaders themselves bowed down before the mob; and for the next two years the state elections were concerned purely with personal politics, the main point at issue in the choice for every United States senator being, whether he would or would not support Benton's expunging resolution. The whole affair seems to us so puerile that we can hardly understand the importance attached to it by the actors themselves. But the men who happened at that period to be the leaders in public affairs were peculiarly and frankly incapable of separating in their minds matters merely affecting themselves from matters affecting their constituents. Each firmly believed that if he was not the whole state, he was at least a most important fraction of it; and this was as plainly seen in Webster's colossal egoism and the frank vanity of Henry Clay as in Benton's ponderous self-consciousness and the all-pervading personality of Andrew Jackson.

Some of the speeches on the expunging resolution show delicious, although entirely unconscious, humor. If there ever was a wholly irrational state of mind it was that in which the Jacksonians perpetually kept themselves. Every canvass on Jackson's behalf was one of sound, fury, and excitement, of appeal to the passions, prejudices, and feelings, but never the reason, of the people. A speech for him was generally a mere frantic denunciation of whatever and whoever was opposed to him, coupled with fulsome adulation of "the old hero." His supporters rarely indeed spoke to the cool judgment of the country, for the very excellent reason that the cool judgment of the country was apt to be against them. Such being the case, it is amusing to read in Benton's speech on receiving the protest the following sentences, apparently uttered in solemn good faith, and with sublime unconsciousness of irony:—

> To such a community [the American body politic]—in an appeal on a great question of constitutional law to the understandings of such a people—declamation, passion, epithets, opprobrious language, will stand for nothing. They will float harmless and unheeded through the empty air, and strike in vain upon the ear of a sober and dispassionate tribunal. Indignation, real or affected; wrath, however hot; fury, however enraged; asseverations, however violent; denunciation, however furious, will avail nothing. Facts, inexorable facts, are all that will be attended to; reason, calm and self-possessed, is all that will be listened to.

The description of the mass of Jacksonian voters as forming "a sober and dispassionate tribunal" is an artistic touch of fancy quite unique, but admirably characteristic of Benton, whose statements always rose vigorously to the necessities of the occasion.

Webster, in an effort to make the best of untoward circumstances, brought in a bill to re-charter the Bank for a short period, at the same time doing away with some of the features that were objectionable in the old charter. This bill might have passed, had it not been opposed by the extreme Bank men, including Clay and Calhoun. In the course of the debate over it Benton delivered a very elaborate and carefully studied speech in favor of hard money and a currency of the precious metals; a speech which is to this day well worth careful reading. Some of his financial theories were crude and confused; but on the main question he was perfectly sound. Both he and Jackson deserve great credit for having done much to impress the popular mind with the benefit of hard, that is to say honest, money. Benton was the strongest hard-money man then in public life, being, indeed, popularly nicknamed "Old Bullion." He thoroughly appreciated that a metallic currency was of more vital importance to the laboring men and to men of small capital generally than to any of the richer classes. A metallic currency is always surer and safer than a paper currency; where it exists a laboring man dependent on his wages need fear less than any other member of the community the evils of bad banking. Benton's idea of the danger to the masses from "the money power" was exaggerated; but in advocating a sound gold currency he took the surest way to overcome any possible dangerous tendency. A craze for "soft," or dishonest, money—a greenback movement, or one for short weight silver dollars—works more to the disadvantage of the whole mass of the people than even to that of the capitalists; it is a move directly in the interests of "the money power," which its loud-mouthed advocates are ostensibly opposing in the interests of democracy.

Benton continued his speeches. The panic was now subsiding; there had not been time for Jackson's ruinous policy of making deposits in numerous state banks, and thereby encouraging wild inflation of credit, to bear fruit and, as it afterwards did, involve the whole country in financial disaster. Therefore Benton was able to exult greatly over the favorable showing of affairs in the report of the secretary of the treasury. He also procured the passage of a gold currency law, which, however, fixed the ratio of value between gold and silver at sixteen to one; an improper proportion, but one which had prevailed for three centuries in the Spanish-American countries, from which he copied it. In consequence of this law gold, long banished, became once more a circulating medium of exchange.

The Bank of the United States afterwards was turned into the State Bank of Pennsylvania; it was badly managed and finally became insolvent. The Jacksonians accepted its downfall as a vindication of their policy; but in reality it was due to causes not operative at the time of the great struggle between the president and the Senate over its continued existence. Certainly by no possible financial policy could it have produced such widespread ruin and distress as did the system introduced by Jackson.

Long after the Bank controversy had lost all practical bearing it continued to be agitated by the chief parties to it, who still felt sore from the various encounters. Jackson assailed it again in his message; a friendly committee of the Senate investigated it and reported in its favor, besides going out of their way to rake up charges against Jackson and Benton. The latter replied in a long speech, and became involved in personalities with the chairman, Tyler of Virginia. Neither side paid attention to any but the partisan aspect of the question, and the discussions were absolutely profitless.

The whole matter was threshed over again and again, long after nothing but chaff was left, during the debates on Benton's expunging resolution. Few now would defend this resolution. The original resolution of censure may have been of doubtful propriety; but it was passed, was entered on the record, and had become a part of the journal of the Senate. It would have been perfectly proper to pass another resolution condemning or reversing the original one, and approving the course of the president; but it was in the highest degree improper to set about what was in form falsifying the record. Still, Benton found plenty of precedents in the annals of other legislative bodies for what he proposed to do, and the country, as a whole, backed him up heartily. He was further stimulated by the knowledge that there was probably no other legislative act in which Jackson took such intense interest, or which could so gratify his pride; the mortification to Clay and Calhoun would be equally great. Benton's motion failed more than once, but the complexion of the Senate was rapidly changed by the various states substituting Democratic for Whig or anti-Jackson senators. Some of the changes were made, as in Virginia, by senators refusing to vote for the expunging resolution, as required by the state legislatures, and then resigning their seats, pursuant to a ridiculous theory of the ultra Democrats, which, if carried out, would completely nullify the provision for a six year's senatorial term. Finally, at the very close of Jackson's administration, Benton found himself with a fair majority behind him, and made the final move. His speech was of course mainly filled with a highly colored account of the blessings wrought for the American people by Andrew Jackson, and equally of course the latter was compared at length to a variety of ancient Roman worthies. The final scene in the Senate had an element of the comic about it. The expungers held a caucus and agreed to sit the session out until the resolution was passed; and with prudent forethought Benton, well aware that when hungry and tired his followers might show less inflexibility of purpose, provided in an adjoining committee-room "an ample supply of cold hams, turkeys, rounds of beef, pickles, wines, and cups of hot coffee," wherewith to inspirit the faint-hearted.

Fortified by the refreshments, the expungers won a complete victory. If the language of Jackson's admirers was overdrawn and strained to the last degree in lauding him for every virtue that he had or had not, it must be remembered that his opponents went quite as far wrong on the other side in their denunciations and extravagant prophecies of gloom. Webster made a very dignified and forcible speech in closing the argument against the resolution, but Calhoun and Clay were much less moderate,—the latter drawing a vivid picture of a rapidly approaching reign of lawless military violence, and asserting that his opponents had "extinguished one of the brightest and purest lights that ever burnt at the altar of civil liberty." As a proper finale Jackson, to show his appreciation, gave a great dinner to the expungers and their wives, Benton sitting at the head of the table. Jackson and Benton solemnly thought that they were taking part in a great act of justice, and were amusingly unable to see the comic side of their acts. They probably really believed most of their own denunciations of the Bank, and very possibly thought that the wickedness of its followers might tempt them to do any desperate deed. At any rate they enjoyed posing alike to themselves and to the public as persons of antique virtue, who had risked both life and reputation in a hazardous but successful attempt to save the liberties of the people from the vast and hostile forces of the aristocratic "money power."

The best verdict on the expunging resolution was given by Webster when he characterized the whole affair as one which, if it were not regarded as a ruthless violation of a sacred instrument, would appear to be little elevated above the character of a contemptible farce.

CHAPTER VII.

THE DISTRIBUTION OF THE SURPLUS.

Benton was supremely self-satisfied with the part he had played in the struggle with the Bank. But very few thinking men would now admit that his actions, as a whole, on the occasion in question, were to his credit, although in the matter of the branch drafts he was perfectly right, and in that of the re-charter at least occupied defensible ground. His general views on monetary matters, however, were sound, and on some of the financial questions that shortly arose he occupied a rather lonely pre-eminence of good sense among his fellow senators; such being particularly the case as regards the various mischievous schemes in relation to disposing of the public lands, and of the money drawn from their sale. The revenue derived from all sources, including these sales of public lands, had for some years been much in excess of the governmental expenses, and a surplus had accumulated in the treasury. This surplus worked more damage than any deficit would have done.

There were gold mines in the Southern States, which had been growing more and more productive; and, as the cost of freighting the bullion was excessive, a bill was introduced to establish branch mints at New Orleans and in the gold regions of Georgia and North Carolina. Benton advocated this strongly, as a constitutional right of the South and West, and as greatly in the interest of those two sections; and also as being another move in favor of a hard-money currency as opposed to one of paper. There was strong opposition to the bill; many of the Whigs having been carried so far by their heated devotion to the United States Bank in its quarrel that they had become paper-money men. But the vote was neither sectional nor partisan in its character. Clay led the opposition, while Webster supported Benton.

Before this time propositions to distribute among the states the revenue from the public lands had become common; and they were succeeded by propositions to distribute the lands themselves, and then by others to distribute all the surplus revenue. Calhoun finally introduced an amendment to the Constitution to enable the surplus in the treasury during the next eight years to be distributed among the various states; the estimate being that for the time mentioned there would be about nine millions surplus annually. Benton attacked the proposal very ably, showing the viciousness of a scheme which would degrade every state government into the position of a mendicant, and would allow money to be collected from the citizens with one hand in order to be given back to them with the other; and also denying that the surplus would reach anything like the dimensions indicated. He ridiculed the idea of making a constitutional amendment to cover so short a period of time; and stated that he would greatly prefer to see the price paid for public lands by incoming settlers reduced, and what surplus there was expended on strengthening the defenses of the United States against foreign powers. This last proposition was eminently proper. We were then, as always, in our chronic state of utter defenselessness against any hostile attack, and yet were in imminent danger of getting embroiled with at least one great power—France. Our danger is always that we shall spend too little, and not too much, in keeping ourselves prepared for foreign war. Calhoun's resolution was a total failure, and was never even brought to a vote.

Benton's proposed method of using the surplus came in with peculiar propriety on account of the conduct of the Whigs and Nullifiers in joining to oppose the appropriation of three millions of dollars for purposes of defense, which was provided for in the general fortification bill. The House passed this bill by a great majority. It was eminently proper that we should at once take steps to provide for the very possible contingency of a war with France, as the relations with that power were growing more threatening every day; but the opposition of the anti-Jackson men to the administration and to all its measures had become so embittered that they were willing to run the risk of seriously damaging the national credit and honor, if they could thereby score a point against their political adversaries. Accordingly, under the lead of Webster, Clay, and Calhoun, they defeated the bill in the Senate, in spite of all that could be done to save it by Benton, who, whatever his faults, was always patriotic. The appropriation had been very irregular in form, and under ordinary circumstances there would have been good justification for inquiring into it before permitting its passage; but under the circumstances its defeat at the moment was most unfortunate. For the president had been pressing France, even to the point of tolerably plain threats, in order to induce or compel her to fulfill the conditions of the recent treaty by which she had bound herself to pay a considerable indemnity, long owing by her to the United States for depredations on our commerce. Now she menaced war, avowedly on the ground that we were unprepared to resist her; and this vote in the Senate naturally led the French government to suppose that Jackson was not sustained by the country in the vigorous position which he had assumed. In speaking on the message of the president which alluded to this state of affairs, Benton strongly advocated our standing firmly for our rights, making a good speech, which showed much historical learning. He severely reproached the anti-administration senators for their previous conduct in causing the loss of the defense appropriation bill, and for preferring to do worse than waste the surplus by distributing it among the different states instead of applying it according to the provisions of that wise measure.

This brought on a bitter wrangle, in which Benton certainly had the best of it. Calhoun was in favor of humiliating non-resistance; he never advocated warlike measures when the dignity of the nation was at stake, fond though he was of threatening violence on behalf of slavery or that form of secession known as nullification. Benton quoted from speeches in the French Chamber of Deputies to show that the French were encouraged to take the position that they did on account of the action of the Senate, and the disposition shown by a majority among the senators rather to pull down the president in a party struggle than to uphold him in his efforts to save the national honor in a contest with France. A curious feature of his speech was that in which he warned the latter power that, in the event of a conflict, it would have to do with a branch of the same race which, "from the days of Agincourt and Crecy, of Blenheim and Ramillies, down to the days of Salamanca and Waterloo, has always known perfectly well how to deal with the impetuous and fiery courage of the French." This sudden out-cropping of what, in Bentonian English, might be called Pan-Anglo-Saxon sentiment was all the more surprising inasmuch as both Benton himself and the party to which he belonged were strongly anti-English in their way of looking at our foreign policy, at least so far as North America was concerned. In the end France yielded, though trying to maintain her dignity by stating that she had not done so, and the United States received what was due them.

Benton strongly opposed the payment by the United States of the private claims of its citizens for damages arising from the French spoliations at the end of the last century. He pointed out that the effort to pay such claims, scores of years after the time of their accruing, rarely benefits any of the parties originally in interest, and can only do real service to dishonest speculators. His speech on this matter would not be bad reading for some of the pension-jobbing congressmen of the present day, and their supporters; but as concerned these French claims he could have been easily answered.

In the controversy over the bill introduced by Clay, to distribute the revenue derived from the public lands among the states for the next five years, Benton showed to great advantage compared both to the introducer of the bill himself, and to Webster, his supporter. He had all along taken the view of the land question that would be natural to a far-seeing Western statesman desirous of encouraging immigration. He wished the public lands to be sold in small parcels to actual settlers, at prices that would allow any poor man who was thrifty to take up a claim. He had already introduced a bill to sell them at graduated prices, the minimum being established at a dollar and twenty-five cents an acre; but if land remained unsold at this rate for three years it was then to be sold for what it would bring in the market. This bill passed the Senate, but failed in the House.

In opposing Clay's distribution scheme Benton again brought forward his plan of using the surplus to provide for the national defenses; and in his speech showed the strongly national turn of his mind, saying:—

In this great system of national defense the whole Union is equally interested; for the country, in all that concerns its defenses, is but a unit, and every section is interested in the defense of every other section, and every individual citizen is interested in the defense of the whole population. It is in vain to say that the navy is on the sea, and the fortifications on the sea-board, and that the citizens in the interior states, or in the valley of the Mississippi, have no interest in these remote defenses. Such an idea is mistaken and delusive; the inhabitant of Missouri or of Indiana has a direct interest in keeping open the mouths of the rivers, defending the sea-port towns, and preserving a naval force that will protect the produce of his labor in crossing the ocean and arriving safely in foreign markets.

Benton's patriotism always included the whole country in spite of the strength of his local sympathies.

The bill passed the Senate by a rather close vote, and went to the House, where it soon become evident that it was doomed to failure. There was another bill, practically of much the same import, before the Senate, providing for the distribution of the surplus among the states in proportion to their electoral votes, but omitting the excellent proviso concerning the defenses. To suit the views of Calhoun and the sticklers for strict construction generally, the form of this rival bill was changed, so that the "distribution" purported to be a "deposit" merely; the money being nominally only loaned to the states, who pledged their faith to return it when Congress should call for it. As it was of course evident that such a loan would never be repaid, the substitution of "deposit" for "distribution" can only be regarded as a verbal change to give the doctrinaires a loop-hole for escape from their previous position; they all took advantage of it, and the bill received overwhelming support, and was passed by both houses.

Benton, however, stood out against it to the last, and in a very powerful speech foretold the evils which the plan would surely work. He scornfully exposed the way in which some of the members were trying, by a trick of wording, to hide the nature of the bill they were enacting into a law, and thus to seem to justify themselves for the support they were giving it. "It is in name a deposit; in form, a loan; in essence and design, a distribution," said Benton. He ridiculed the attitude of the hair-splitting strict constructionists, like Calhoun, who had always pretended most scrupulously to respect the exact wording of the Constitution, and who had previously refused to vote for distribution on the ground that it was unconstitutional:—

At the commencement of the present session a proposition was made [by Calhoun] to amend the Constitution, to permit this identical distribution to be made. That proposition is now upon our calendar, for the action of Congress. All at once it is discovered that a change of name will do as well as a change of the Constitution. Strike out the word "distribute" and insert the word "deposit," and incontinently the impediment is removed; the constitutional difficulty is surmounted, and the distribution can be made.

He showed that to the states themselves the moneys distributed would either be useless, or else—and much more probably—they would be fruitful sources of corruption and political debauchery. He was quite right. It would have been very much better to have destroyed the surplus than to have distributed it as was actually done. None of the states gained any real benefit by the transaction; most were seriously harmed. At the best, the money was squandered in the rage for public improvements that then possessed the whole people; often it was stolen outright, or never accounted for. In the one case, it was an incentive to extravagance; in the other, it was a corruption fund. Yet the popular feeling was strongly in favor of the measure at the time, and Benton was almost the only public man of note who dared to resist it. On this occasion, as in the closing act of the struggle with the Nullifiers, he showed more backbone than did his great chief; for Jackson signed the bill, although criticising it most forcibly and pungently.

The success of this measure naturally encouraged the presentation of others. Clay attempted to revive his land-money distribution bill, but was defeated, mainly through Benton's efforts. Three or four other similar schemes, including one of Calhoun's, also failed. Finally a clause providing for a further "deposit" of surplus moneys with the states was tacked to a bill appropriating money for defenses, thereby loading it down so that it was eventually lost. In the Senate the "deposit" amendment was finally struck out, in spite of the opposition of Clay, Calhoun, and Webster. Throughout the whole discussion of the distribution of the surplus Benton certainly shines by comparison with any one of his three great senatorial rivals.

He shows to equally great advantage compared to them in the part taken by him in reference to Jackson's so-called specie circulars. The craze for speculation had affected the sales of public lands, which were increasing at an extraordinary rate, nearly twenty-five million dollars' worth being sold in 1836. As a rule, the payments were made in the notes of irresponsible banks, gotten up in many cases by the land speculators themselves. The sales were running up to five millions a month, with prospect of a boundless increase, so that all the public land bade fair to be converted into inconvertible paper. Benton had foreseen the evil results attending such a change, and, though well aware that he was opposing powerful interests in his own section of the country, had already tried to put a stop to it by law. In his speech he had stated that the unprecedented increase in the sale of public lands was due to the accommodations received by speculators from worthless banks, whose notes in small denominations would be taken to some distant part of the country, whence it would be a long time before they were returned and presented for payment. The speculators, with paper of which the real value was much below par, could outbid settlers and cultivators who could only offer specie, or notes that were its equivalent. He went on to say that "the effect was equally injurious to every interest concerned—except the banks and the speculators: it was injurious to the treasury, which was filling up with paper; to the new states, which were flooded with paper; and to settlers and cultivators, who were outbid by speculators loaded with this borrowed paper. A return to specie payments for lands was the remedy for all these evils."

Benton's reasoning was perfectly sound. The effects on settlers, on the new states, and on the government itself were precisely such as he described, and the proposed remedy was the right one. But his bill failed; for the Whigs, including even Webster, had by this time worked themselves up until they were fairly crazy at the mere mention of paper-money banks.

Jackson, however, not daunted by the fate of the bill, got Benton to draw up a treasury order, and had it issued. This served the same purpose, as it forbade the land-offices to receive anything but gold and silver in payment for land. It was not issued until Congress had adjourned, for fear that body might counteract it by a law; and this was precisely what was attempted at the next session, when a joint resolution was passed rescinding the order, and practically endeavoring to impose the worthless paper currency of the states upon the federal government. Benton stood almost alone in the fight he made against this resolution, although the right of the matter was so plainly on his side. In his speech he foretold clearly the coming of the great financial crisis that was then near at hand. The resolution, however, amounted to nothing, as it turned out, for it was passed so late in the session that the president, by simply withholding his signature from it, was enabled to prevent it from having effect.

CHAPTER VIII.

THE SLAVE QUESTION APPEARS IN POLITICS.

Towards the close of Jackson's administration, slavery for the first time made its permanent appearance in national politics; although for some years yet it had little or no influence in shaping the course of political movements. In 1833 the abolition societies of the North came into prominence; they had been started a couple of years previously.

Black slavery was such a grossly anachronistic and un-American form of evil, that it is difficult to discuss calmly the efforts to abolish it, and to remember that many of these efforts were calculated to do, and actually did, more harm than good. We are also very apt to forget that it was perfectly possible and reasonable for enlightened and virtuous men, who fully recognized it as an evil, yet to prefer its continuance to having it interfered with in a way that would produce even worse results. Black slavery in Hayti was characterized by worse abuse than ever was the case in the United States; yet, looking at the condition of that republic now, it may well be questioned whether it would not have been greatly to her benefit in the end to have had slavery continue a century or so longer,—its ultimate extinction being certain,— rather than to have had her attain freedom as she actually did, with the results that have flowed from her action. When an evil of colossal size exists, it is often the case that there is no possible way of dealing with it that will not itself be fraught with baleful results. Nor can the ultra-philanthropic method be always, or even often, accepted as the best. If there is one question upon which the philanthropists of the present day, especially the more emotional ones, are agreed, it is that any law restricting Chinese immigration is an outrage; yet it seems incredible that any man of even moderate intelligence should not see that no greater calamity could now befall the United States than to have the Pacific slope fill up with a Mongolian population.

The cause of the Abolitionists has had such a halo shed round it by the after course of events, which they themselves in reality did very little to shape, that it has been usual to speak of them with absurdly exaggerated praise. Their courage, and for the most part their sincerity, cannot be too highly spoken of, but their share in abolishing slavery was far less than has commonly been represented; any single non-abolitionist politician, like Lincoln or Seward, did more than all the professional Abolitionists combined really to bring about its destruction. The abolition societies were only in a very restricted degree the causes of the growing feeling in the North against slavery; they are rather to be regarded as themselves manifestations or accompaniments of that feeling. The anti-slavery outburst in the Northern States over the admission of Missouri took place a dozen years before there was an abolition society in existence; and the influence of the professional abolitionists upon the growth of the anti-slavery sentiment as often as not merely warped it and twisted it out of proper shape,—as when at one time they showed a strong inclination to adopt disunion views, although it was self-evident that by no possibility could slavery be abolished unless the Union was preserved. Their tendency towards impracticable methods was well shown in the position they assumed towards him who was not only the greatest American, but also the greatest man, of the nineteenth century; for during all the terrible four years that sad, strong, patient Lincoln worked and suffered for the people, he had to dread the influence of the extreme Abolitionists only less than that of the Copperheads. Many of their leaders possessed no good qualities beyond their fearlessness and truth—qualities that were also possessed by the Southern fire-eaters. They belonged to that class of men that is always engaged in some agitation or other; only it happened that in this particular agitation they were right. Wendell Phillips may be taken as a very good type of the whole. His services against slavery prior to the war should always be remembered with gratitude; but after the war, and until the day of his death, his position on almost every public question was either mischievous or ridiculous, and usually both.

When the abolitionist movement started it was avowedly designed to be cosmopolitan in character; the originators looked down upon any merely national or patriotic feeling. This again deservedly took away from their influence. In fact, it would have been most unfortunate had the majority of the Northerners been from the beginning in hearty accord with the Abolitionists; at the best it would have resulted at that time in the disruption of the Union and the perpetuation of slavery in the South.

But after all is said, the fact remains, that on the main issue the Abolitionists were at least working in the right direction. Sooner or later, by one means or another, slavery had to go. It is beyond doubt a misfortune that in certain districts the bulk of the population should be composed of densely ignorant negroes, often criminal or vicious in their instincts; but such is the case, and the best, and indeed the only proper course to pursue, is to treat them with precisely the same justice that is meted out to whites. The effort to do so in time immediately past has not resulted so successfully as was hoped and expected; but nevertheless no other way would have worked as well.

Slavery was chiefly responsible for the streak of coarse and brutal barbarism which ran through the Southern character, and which marked the ferocious outcry instantly raised by the whole Southern press against the Abolitionists. There had been an abortive negro rising in Virginia almost at the same time that the abolitionist movement first came into prominence; and this fact added to the rage and terror with which the South regarded the latter. The clamor against the North was deafening; and though it soon subsided for the time being, it never afterwards entirely died away. As has been shown already, there had always been a strong separatist feeling in the South; but hitherto its manifestations had been local and sporadic, never affecting all the states at the same time; for it had never happened that the cause which called forth any particular manifestation was one bearing on the whole South alike. The alien and sedition laws were more fiercely resented in Virginia and Kentucky than in South Carolina; the tariff, which so angered the latter, pleased Louisiana; and Georgia and Alabama alone were affected by the presence of great Indian communities within their borders. But slavery was an interest common to the whole South. When it was felt to be in any way menaced, all Southerners came together for its protection; and, from the time of the rise of the Abolitionists onward, the separatist movement throughout the South began to identify itself with the maintenance of slavery, and gradually to develop greater and greater strength. Its growth was furthered and hastened by the actions of the more ambitious and unscrupulous of the Southern politicians, who saw that it offered a chance for them to push themselves forward, and who were perfectly willing to wreak almost irreparable harm to the nation if by so doing they could advance their own selfish interests. It was in reference to these politicians that Benton quoted with approval a letter from ex-President Madison, which ran:—

> The danger is not to be concealed, that the sympathy arising from known causes, and the inculcated impression of a permanent incompatibility of interests between the South and the North may put it in the power of popular leaders, aspiring to the highest stations, to unite the South, on some critical occasion, in a course that will end by creating a new theatre of great, though inferior, interest. In pursuing this course the first and most obvious step is nullification, the next secession, and the last a farewell separation.

This was a pretty good forecast of the crisis that was precipitated by the greedy and reckless ambition of the secessionist leaders in 1860. The moral difference between Benedict Arnold on the one hand, and Aaron Burr or Jefferson Davis on the other, is precisely the difference that obtains between a politician who sells his vote for money and one who supports a bad measure in consideration of being given some high political position.

The Abolitionists immediately contrived to bring themselves before the notice of Congress in two ways; by the presentation of petitions for the abolition of slavery in the District of Columbia, and by sending out to the Southern States a shoal of abolition pamphlets, newspapers, and rather ridiculous illustrated cuts. What the precise point of the last proceeding was no one can tell; the circulation of such writings as theirs in the South could not possibly serve any good purpose. But they had a right to send what they wished, and the conduct of many of the Southerners in trying to get a federal law passed to prohibit their writings from being carried in the mail was as wrong as it was foolish; while the brutal clamor raised in the South against the whole North as well as against the Abolitionists, and the conduct of certain Southern legislatures in practically setting prices on the heads of the leaders in the objectionable movement, in turn angered the North and gave the Abolitionists ten-fold greater strength than they would otherwise have had.

The question first arose upon the presentation of a perfectly proper and respectful petition sent to the Senate by a society of Pennsylvania Quakers, and praying for the abolition of slavery in the District of Columbia. The District was solely under the control of Congress, and was the property of the nation at large, so that Congress was the proper and the only body to which any petition concerning the affairs of the District could be sent; and if the right of petition meant anything, it certainly meant that the people, or any portion thereof, should have the right to petition their representatives in regard to their own affairs. Yet certain Southern extremists, under the lead of Calhoun, were anxious to refuse to receive the paper. Benton voted in favor of receiving it, and was followed in his action by a number of other Southern senators. He spoke at length on the subject, and quite moderately, even crediting the petitioners, or many of them, with being "good people, aiming at benevolent objects, and endeavoring to ameliorate the condition of one part of the human race, without inflicting calamities on another part," which was going very far indeed for a slave-holding senator of that time. He was of course totally opposed to abolition and the Abolitionists, and showed that the only immediate effect of the movement had been to make the lot of the slaves still worse, and for the moment to do away with any chance of intelligently discussing the question of emancipation. For, like many other Southerners, he fondly cherished the idea of gradual peaceful emancipation,—an idea which the course of events made wholly visionary, but which, under the circumstances, might well have been realized. He proceeded to give most questionable praise to the North for some acts as outrageous and disgraceful as were ever perpetrated by its citizens, stating that—

> Their conduct was above all praise, above all thanks, above all gratitude. They had chased off the foreign emissaries, silenced the gabbling tongues of female dupes, and dispersed the assemblages, whether fanatical, visionary, or incendiary, of all that congregated to preach against evils that affected others, not themselves; and to propose remedies to aggravate the disease which they had pretended to cure. They had acted with a noble spirit. They had exerted

a vigor beyond all law. They had obeyed the enactments,
not of the statute-book, but of the heart.

These fervent encomiums were fully warranted by the acts of various
Northern mobs, that had maltreated abolitionist speakers, broken up anti-
slavery meetings, and committed numerous other deeds of lawless violence.
But however flattered the Northerners of that generation may have been, in
feeling that they thoroughly deserved Benton's eulogy, it is doubtful if their
descendants will take quite the same pride in looking back to it. An amusing
incident of the debate was Calhoun's attack upon one of the most subservient
allies the South ever had in the Northern States; he caused to be sent up to
the desk and read an abolition paper published in New Hampshire, which
contained a bitter assault upon Franklin Pierce, then a member of Congress.
Nominally he took this course to show that there was much greater strength
in the abolition movement, and therefore much greater danger to the South,
than the Northern senators were willing to admit; in reality he seems to have
acted partly from wanton malice, partly from overbearing contempt for the
truckling allies and apologists of slavery in the North, and partly from a desire
not to see the discussion die out, but rather, in spite of his continual
profession to the contrary, to see it maintained as a standing subject of
irritation. He wished to refuse to receive the petitions, on the ground that
they touched a subject that ought not even to be discussed; yet he must have
known well that he was acting in the very way most fitted to give rise to
discussion,—a fact that was pointed out to him by Benton, in a caustic
speech. He also took the ground that the question of emancipation affected
the states exclusively, and that Congress had no more jurisdiction over the
subject in the District of Columbia than she had in the State of North
Carolina. This precious contribution to the true interpretation of the
Constitution was so farcically and palpably false that it is incredible that he
should himself have believed what he was saying. He was still smarting from
the nullification controversy; he had seceded from his party, and was sore
with disappointed ambition; and it seems very improbable that he was honest
in his professions of regret at seeing questions come up which would disturb
the Union. On the contrary, much of the opposition he was continually
making to supposititious federal and Northern encroachments on the rights
of the South must have been merely factious, and it seems likely that, partly
from a feeling of revenge and partly with the hope of gratifying his ambition,
he was anxious to do all he could to work the South up to the highest pitch
of irritation, and keep her there until there was a dissolution of the Union.
Benton evidently thought that this was the case; and in reading the constant
threats of nullification and secession which run through all Calhoun's
speeches, and the innumerable references he makes to the alleged fact that
he had come off victorious in his treasonable struggle over the tariff in 1833,
it is difficult not to accept Benton's view of the matter. He always spoke of

Calhoun with extreme aversion, and there were probably moments when he was inclined heartily to sympathize with Jackson's death-bed regret that he had not hung the South Carolina Nullifier. Doubtless in private life, or as regards any financial matters, Calhoun's conduct was always blameless; but it may well be that he has received far more credit for purity of motive in his public conduct than his actions fairly entitle him to.

Calhoun was also greatly exercised over the circulation of abolition documents in the South. At his request a committee of five was appointed to draft a bill on the subject; he was chairman, and three of the other four members were from the Slave States; yet his report was so extreme that only one of the latter would sign it with him. He introduced into it a long argument to the effect that the Constitution was a mere compact between sovereign states, and inferentially that nullification and secession were justifiable and constitutional; and then drew a vivid picture of the unspeakable horrors with which, as he contended, the action of the Northern Abolitionists menaced the South. The bill subjected to penalties any postmaster who should knowingly receive and put into the mail any publication touching slavery, to go into any state which had forbidden by law the circulation of such a publication. In discussing this bill he asserted that Congress, in refusing to pass it, would be coöperating with the Abolitionists; and then he went on to threaten as usual that in such case nullification or secession would become necessary. Benton had become pretty well tired of these threats, his attachment to the Union even exceeding his dislike to seeing slavery meddled with; and he headed the list of half a dozen Southern senators who joined with the bulk of the Northerners in defeating the bill, which was lost by a vote of twenty-five to nineteen. A few of the Northern "dough-faces" voted with Calhoun. There is a painfully striking contrast between the courage shown by Benton, a slave-holder with a slave-holding constituency, in opposing this bill, and the obsequious subserviency to the extreme Southern feeling shown on the same occasion by Wright, Van Buren, and Buchanan—fit representatives of the sordid and odious political organizations of New York and Pennsylvania.

Several other questions came up towards the end of Jackson's administration which were more or less remotely affected by the feeling about slavery. Benton succeeded in getting a bill through to extend the boundaries of the State of Missouri so as to take in territory lying northwest of her previous limit, the Indian title to which was extinguished by treaty. This annexed land lay north of the boundary for slave territory established by the Missouri Compromise; but Benton experienced no difficulty in getting his bill through. It was not, however, in the least a move designed in the interests of the slave power. Missouri's feeling was precisely that which would actuate

Oregon or Washington Territory to-day, if either wished to annex part of Northern Idaho.

The territories of Arkansas and Michigan had applied for admission into the Union as states; and as one would be a free and the other a slave state, it was deemed proper that they should come in together. Benton himself urged the admission of the free state of Michigan, while the interests of Arkansas were confided to Buchanan of Pennsylvania. The slavery question entered but little into the matter; although some objections were raised on that score, as well as on account of the irregular manner in which the would-be states had acted in preparing for admission. The real ground of opposition to the admission of the two new states was political, as it was known that they could both be relied upon for Democratic majorities at the approaching presidential election. Many Whigs, therefore, both from the North and the South, opposed it.

The final removal of the Cherokees from Georgia and Alabama was brought about in 1836 by means of a treaty with those Indians. Largely through the instrumentality of Benton, and in spite of the opposition of Clay, Calhoun, and Webster, this instrument was ratified in the Senate by the close vote of thirty-one to fifteen. Although new slave territory was thus acquired, the vote on the treaty was factional and not sectional, being equally divided between the Northern and the Southern States, Calhoun and six other Southern senators opposing it, chiefly from hostility to the administration. The removal of the Indians was probably a necessity; undoubtedly it worked hardship in individual instances, but on the whole it did not in the least retard the civilization of the tribe, which was fully paid for its losses; and moreover, in its new home, continued to make progress in every way until it became involved in the great civil war, and received a setback from which it has not yet recovered. These Cherokees were almost the last Indians left in any number east of the Mississippi, and their removal solved the Indian problem so far as the old states were concerned.

Later on Benton went to some trouble to disprove the common statement that we have robbed the original Indian occupants of their lands. He showed by actual statistics that up to 1840 we had paid to the Indians eighty-five millions of dollars for land purchases, which was over five times as much as the United States gave the great Napoleon for Louisiana; and about three times as much as we paid France, Spain, and Mexico together for the purchase of Louisiana, Florida, and California; while the amount of land received in return would not equal any one of these purchases, and was but a fractional part of Louisiana or California. We paid the Cherokees for their territory exactly as much as we paid the French, at the height of their power, for Louisiana; while as to the Creek and Choctaw nations, we paid each more for their lands than we paid for Louisiana and Florida combined. The dealings of the government with the Indian have often been unwise, and sometimes unjust; but they are very far indeed from being so black as is commonly represented, especially when the tremendous difficulties of the case are taken into account.

Far more important than any of these matters was the acknowledgment of the independence of Texas; and in this, as well as in the troubles with Mexico which sprang from it, slavery again played a prominent part, although not nearly so important at first as has commonly been represented. Doubtless the slave-holders worked hard to secure additional territory out of which to form new slave states; but Texas and California would have been in the end taken by us, had there not been a single slave in the Mississippi valley. The greed for the conquest of new lands which characterized the Western people had nothing whatever to do with the fact that some of them owned slaves. Long before there had been so much as the faintest foreshadowing of the importance which the slavery question was to assume, the West had been eagerly pressing on to territorial conquest, and had been chafing and fretting at the restraint put upon it, and at the limits set to its strivings by the treaties established with foreign powers. The first settlers beyond the Alleghanies, and their immediate successors, who moved down along the banks of the Ohio, the Cumberland, and the Tennessee, and thence out to the Mississippi itself, were not generally slave-holders; but they were all as anxious to wrest the Mississippi valley from the control of the French as their descendants were to overrun the Spanish lands lying along the Rio Grande. In other words, slavery had very little to do with the Western aggressions on Mexican territory, however it might influence the views of Southern statesmen as to lending support to the Western schemes.

The territorial boundaries of all the great powers originally claiming the soil of the West—France, Spain, and the United States—were very ill-defined, there being no actual possession of the lands in dispute, and each power making a great showing on its own map. If the extreme views of any one were admitted, its adversary, for the time being, would have had nothing. Thus before the treaty of 1819 with Spain our nominal boundaries and those of the latter power in the West overlapped each other; and the extreme Western men persisted in saying that we had given up some of the territory which belonged to us because we had consented to adopt a middle line of division, and had not insisted upon being allowed the full extent of our claims. Benton always took this view of it, insisting that we had given up our rights by the adoption of this treaty. Many Southerners improved on this idea, and spoke of the desirability of "re-annexing" the territory we had surrendered,—endeavoring by the use of this very inappropriate word to give a color of right to their proceedings. As a matter of fact it was inevitable, as well as in the highest degree desirable for the good of humanity at large, that the American people should ultimately crowd out the Mexicans from their sparsely populated Northern provinces. But it was quite as desirable that this should not be done in the interests of slavery.

American settlers had begun to press into the outlying Spanish province of Texas before the treaty of 1819 was ratified. Their numbers went on increasing, and at first the Mexican government, having achieved independence of Spain, encouraged their incoming. But it soon saw that their presence boded danger, and forbade further immigration; without effect, however, as the settlers and adventurers came thronging in as fast as ever. The Americans had brought their slaves with them, and when the Mexican government issued a decree liberating all slaves, they refused to be bound by it; and this decree was among the reasons alleged for their revolt. It has been represented as the chief if not the sole cause of the rebellion; but in reality it was not the cause at all; it was merely one of the occasions. Long before slavery had been abolished in Mexico, and before it had become an exciting question in the United States, the infant colony of Texas, when but a few months old, had made an abortive attempt at insurrection. Any one who has ever been on the frontier, and who knows anything whatever of the domineering, masterful spirit and bitter race prejudices of the white frontiersmen, will acknowledge at once that it was out of the question that the Texans should long continue under Mexican rule; and it would have been a great misfortune if they had. It was out of the question to expect them to submit to the mastery of the weaker race, which they were supplanting. Whatever might be the pretexts alleged for revolt, the real reasons were to be found in the deeply-marked difference of race, and in the absolute unfitness of the Mexicans then to govern themselves, to say nothing of governing others. During the dozen years that the American colony in Texas formed part of Mexico, the government of the latter went through revolution after revolution,—republic, empire, and military dictatorship following one another in bewildering succession. A state of things like this in the central government, especially when the latter belonged to a race alien in blood, language, religion, and habits of life, would warrant any community in determining to shift for itself. Such would probably have been the result even on people as sober and peaceable as the Texan settlers were warlike, reckless, and overbearing.

But the majority of those who fought for Texan independence were not men who had already settled in that territory, but, on the contrary, were adventurers from the States, who had come to help their kinsmen and to win for themselves, by their own prowess, homes on what was then Mexican soil. It may as well be frankly admitted that the conduct of the American frontiersmen all through this contest can be justified on no possible plea of international morality or law. Still, we cannot judge them by the same standard we should apply to the dealings between highly civilized powers of approximately the same grade of virtue and intelligence. Two nations may be contemporaneous so far as mere years go, and yet, for all that, may be existing among surroundings which practically are centuries apart. The nineteenth century on the banks of the Thames, the Seine, and the Rhine, or even of the Hudson and the Potomac, was one thing; the nineteenth century in the valley of the Rio Grande was another and quite a different thing.

The conquest of Texas should properly be classed with conquests like those of the Norse sea-rovers. The virtues and faults alike of the Texans were those of a barbaric age. They were restless, brave, and eager for adventure, excitement, and plunder; they were warlike, resolute, and enterprising; they had all the marks of a young and hardy race, flushed with the pride of strength and self-confidence. On the other hand they showed again and again the barbaric vies of boastfulness, ignorance, and cruelty; and they were utterly careless of the rights of others, looking upon the possessions of all weaker races as simply their natural prey. A band of settlers entering Texas was troubled by no greater scruples of conscience than, a thousand years before, a ship-load of Knut's followers might have felt at landing in England; and when they were engaged in warfare with the Mexicans they could count with certainty upon assistance from their kinsfolk who had been left behind, and for the same reasons that had enabled Rolf's Norsemen on the sea-coast of France to rely confidently on Scandinavian help in their quarrels with their Karling over-lords. The great Texan hero, Houston, who drank hard and fought hard, who was mighty in battle and crafty in council, with his reckless, boastful courage and his thirst for changes and risks of all kinds, his propensity for private brawling, and his queerly blended impulses for good and evil, might, with very superficial alterations of character, stand as the type of an old-world Viking—plus the virtue of a deep and earnestly patriotic attachment to his whole country. Indeed his career was as picturesque and romantic as that of Harold Hardraada himself, and, to boot, was much more important in its results.

Thus the Texan struggle for independence stirred up the greatest sympathy and enthusiasm in the United States. The administration remained nominally neutral, but obviously sympathized with the Texans, permitting arms and men to be sent to their help, without hindrance, and indeed doing not a little discreditable bullying in the diplomatic dealing with Mexico, which that unfortunate community had her hands too full to resent. Still we did not commit a more flagrant breach of neutrality than, for instance, England was at the same time engaged in committing in reference to the civil wars in Spain. The victory of San Jacinto, in which Houston literally annihilated a Mexican force twice the strength of his own, virtually decided the contest; and the Senate at once passed a resolution recognizing the independence of Texas.

Calhoun wished that body to go farther, and forthwith admit Texas as a state into the Union; but Benton and his colleagues were not prepared to take such a step at so early a date, although intending of course that in the end she should be admitted. There was little opposition to the recognition of Texan independence, although a few members of the lower house, headed by Adams, voted against it. While a cabinet officer, and afterwards as president, Adams had done all that he could to procure by purchase or treaty the very land which was afterwards the cause of our troubles with Mexico.

Much the longest and most elaborate speech in favor of the recognition of Texan independence was made by Benton, to whom the subject appealed very strongly. He announced emphatically that he spoke as a Western senator, voicing the feeling of the West; and he was right. The opposition to the growth of our country on its southwestern frontier was almost confined to the Northeast; the West as a whole, free states as well as slave, heartily favored the movement. The settlers of Texas had come mainly, it is true, from the slave states; but there were also many who had been born north of the Ohio. It was a matter of comment that the guns used at San Jacinto had come from Cincinnati—and so had some of those who served them.

In Benton's speech he began by pointing out the impropriety of doing what Calhoun had done in attempting to complicate the question of the recognition of Texan independence with the admission of Texas as a state. He then proceeded to claim for us a good deal more credit than we were entitled to for our efforts to preserve neutrality; drew a very true picture of the commercial bonds that united us to Mexico, and of the necessity that they should not be lightly broken; gave a spirited sketch of the course of the war hitherto, condemning without stint the horrible butcheries committed by the Mexicans, but touching gingerly on the savage revenge taken by the Americans in their turn; and ended by a eulogy of the Texans themselves, and their leaders.

It was the age of "spread-eagle" speeches, and many of Benton's were no exception to the rule. As a people we were yet in a condition of raw, crude immaturity; and our very sensitiveness to foreign criticism—a sensitiveness which we now find it difficult to understand—and the realization of our own awkwardness made us inclined to brag about and exaggerate our deeds. Our public speakers and writers acquired the abominable habit of speaking of everything and everybody in the United States in the superlative; and therefore, as we claimed the highest rank for all our fourth-rate men, we put it out of our power to do justice to the really first-rate ones; and on account of our continual exaggerations we were not believed by others, and hardly even believed ourselves, when we presented estimates that were truthful. When every public speaker was declared to be a Demosthenes or a Cicero, people failed to realize that we actually had, in Webster, the greatest orator of the century; and when every general who whipped an Indian tribe was likened to Napoleon, we left ourselves no words with which properly to characterize the really heroic deeds done from time to time in the grim frontier warfare. All Benton's oratory took on this lurid coloring; and in the present matter his final eulogy of the Texan warriors was greatly strained, though it would hardly have been in his power to pay too high a tribute to some of the deeds they had done. It was the heroic age of the Southwest; though, as with every other heroic age, there were plenty of failings, vices, and weaknesses visible, if the stand-point of observation was only close enough.

CHAPTER IX.

THE CHILDREN'S TEETH ARE SET ON EDGE.

In his dealings with the Bank and his disposal of the deposits Jackson ate sour grapes to his heart's content; and now the teeth of his adopted child Van Buren were to be set on edge.

Van Buren was the first product of what are now called "machine politics" that was put into the presidential chair. He owed his elevation solely to his own dexterous political manipulation, and to the fact that, for his own selfish ends, and knowing perfectly well their folly, he had yet favored or connived at all the actions into which the administration had been led either through Jackson's ignorance and violence, or by the crafty unscrupulousness and limited knowledge of the Kitchen Cabinet. The people at large would never have thought of him for president of their own accord; but he had become Jackson's political legatee, partly because he had personally endeared himself to the latter, and partly because the politicians felt that he was a man whom they could trust. The Jacksonian Democracy was already completely ruled by a machine, of which the most important cogs were the countless office-holders, whom the spoils system had already converted into a band of well-drilled political mercenaries. A political machine can only be brought to a state of high perfection in a party containing very many ignorant and uneducated voters; and the Jacksonian Democracy held in its ranks the mass of the ignorance of the country. Besides this such an organization requires, in order that it may do its most effective work, to have as its leader and figure-head a man who really has a great hold on the people at large, and who yet can be managed by such politicians as possess the requisite adroitness; and Jackson fulfilled both these conditions. The famous Kitchen Cabinet was so called because its members held no official positions, and yet were known to have Jackson more under their influence than was the case with his nominal advisers. They stood as the first representatives of a type common enough afterwards, and of which Thurlow Weed was perhaps the best example. They were men who held no public position, and yet devoted their whole time to politics, and pulled the strings in obedience to which the apparent public leaders moved.

Jackson liked Van Buren because the latter had served him both personally and politically—indeed Jackson was incapable of distinguishing between a political and a personal service. This liking, however, would not alone have advanced Van Buren's interests, if the latter, who was himself a master in the New York state machine, had not also succeeded in enlisting the good-will and self-interest of the members of the Kitchen Cabinet and the other intimate advisers of the president. These first got Jackson himself thoroughly committed to Van Buren, and then used his name and enormous influence with the masses, coupled with their own mastery of machine methods, to bring about the New Yorker's nomination. In both these moves they had been helped, and Van Buren's chances had been immensely improved, by an incident that had seemed at the time very unfortunate for the latter. When he was secretary of state, in carrying on negotiations with Great Britain relative to the West India trade, he had so far forgotten what was due to the dignity of the nation as to allude disparagingly, while thus communicating with a foreign power, to the course pursued by the previous administration. This extension of party lines into our foreign diplomacy was discreditable to the whole country. The anti-administration men bitterly resented it, and emphasized their resentment by rejecting the nomination of Van Buren when Jackson wished to make him minister to England. Their action was perfectly proper, and Van Buren, by right, should have suffered for his undignified and unpatriotic conduct. But instead of this, and in accordance with the eternal unfitness of things, what really happened was that his rejection by the Senate actually helped him; for Jackson promptly made the quarrel his own, and the masses blindly followed their idol. Benton exultingly and truthfully said that the president's foes had succeeded in breaking a minister only to make a president.

Van Buren faithfully served the mammon of unrighteousness, both in his own state and, later on, at Washington; and he had his reward, for he was advanced to the highest offices in the gift of the nation. He had no reason to blame his own conduct for his final downfall; he got just as far along as he could possibly get; he succeeded because of, and not in spite of, his moral shortcomings; if he had always governed his actions by a high moral standard he would probably never have been heard of. Still, there is some comfort in reflecting that, exactly as he was made president for no virtue of his own, but simply on account of being Jackson's heir, so he was turned out of the office, not for personal failure, but because he was taken as scapegoat, and had the sins of his political fathers visited on his own head.

The opposition to the election of Van Buren was very much disorganized, the Whig party not yet having solidified,—indeed it always remained a somewhat fluid body. The election did not have the slightest sectional significance, slavery not entering into it, and both Northern and Southern States voting without the least reference to the geographical belongings of the candidates. He was the last true Jacksonian Democrat—Union Democrat—who became president; the South Carolina separatists and many of their fellows refused to vote for him. The Democrats who came after him, on the contrary, all had leanings to the separatist element which so soon obtained absolute control of the party, to the fierce indignation of men like Benton, Houston, and the other old Jacksonians, whose sincere devotion to the Union will always entitle them to the gratitude of every true American. As far as slavery was concerned, however, the Southerners had hitherto had nothing whatever to complain of in Van Buren's attitude. He was careful to inform them in his inaugural address that he would not sanction any attempt to interfere with the institution, whether by abolishing it in the District of Columbia or in any other way distasteful to the South. He also expressed a general hope that he would be able throughout to follow in the footsteps of Jackson.

He had hardly been elected before the ruinous financial policy to which he had been party, but of which the effects, it must in justice be said, were aggravated by many of the actions of the Whigs, began to bear fruit after its kind. The use made of the surplus was bad enough, but the withdrawal of the United States deposits from one responsible bank and their distribution among scores of others, many of which were in the most rickety condition, was a step better calculated than any other to bring about a financial crash. It gave a stimulus to extravagance, and evoked the wildest spirit of speculation that the country had yet seen. The local banks, to whom the custody of the public moneys had been intrusted, used them as funds which they and their customers could hazard for the chance of gain; and the gambling spirit, always existent in the American mercantile community, was galvanized into furious life. The public dues were payable in the paper of these deposit banks and of the countless others that were even more irresponsible. The deposit banks thus became filled up with a motley mass of more or less worthless bank paper, which thus formed the "surplus," of which the distribution had caused Congress so much worry. Their condition was desperate, as they had been managed with the most reckless disregard for the morrow. Many of them had hardly kept as much specie in hand as would amount to one fiftieth of the aggregate of their deposits and other immediate liabilities.

The people themselves were of course primarily responsible for the then existing state of affairs; but the government had done all in its power to make matters worse. Panics were certain to occur more or less often in so speculative and venturesome a mercantile community, where there was such heedless trust in the future and such recklessness in the use of credit. But the government, by its actions, immensely increased the severity of this particular panic, and became the prime factor in precipitating its advent. Benton tried to throw the blame mainly on the bankers and politicians, who, he alleged, had formed an alliance for the overthrow of the administration; but he made the plea more half-heartedly than usual, and probably in his secret soul acknowledged its puerility.

The mass of the people were still happy in the belief that all things were working well, and that their show of unexampled prosperity and business activity denoted a permanent and healthy condition. Yet all the signs pointed to a general collapse at no distant date; an era of general bank suspensions, of depreciated currency, and of insolvency of the federal treasury was at hand. No one but Benton, however, seemed able to read the signs aright, and his foreboding utterances were laughed at or treated with scorn by his fellow statesmen. He recalled the memory of the times of 1818-19, when the treasury reports of one year showed a superfluity of revenue of which there was no want, and those of the next showed a deficit which required to be relieved by a loan; and he foretold an infinitely worse result from the inflation of the paper system, saying:—

> Are we not at this moment, and from the same cause, realizing the first part—the elusive and treacherous part— of this picture? and must not the other, the sad and real sequel, speedily follow? The day of revulsion in its effects may be more or less disastrous; but come it must. The present bloat in the paper system cannot continue; violent contraction must follow enormous expansion; a scene of distress and suffering must ensue—to come of itself out of the present state of things, without being stimulated and helped on by our unwise legislation.... *I am one of those who promised gold, not paper; I did not join in putting down the Bank of the United States to put up a wilderness of local banks. I did not join in putting down the currency of a national bank to put up a national paper currency of a thousand local banks.* I did not strike Cæsar to make Antony master of Rome.

These last sentences referred to the passage of the act repealing the specie circular and making the notes of the banks receivable in payment of federal dues. The act was most mischievous, and Benton's criticisms both of it and of the great Whig senator who pressed it were perfectly just; but they apply with quite as much weight to Jackson's dealings with the deposits, which Benton had defended.

Benton foresaw the coming of the panic so clearly, and was so particularly uneasy about the immediate effects upon the governmental treasury, that he not only spoke publicly on the matter in the Senate, but even broached the subject in the course of a private conversation with the president-elect, to get him to try to make what preparations he could. Van Buren, cool, skillful, and far-sighted politician though he was, on this occasion showed that he was infected with the common delusion as to the solidity of the country's business prosperity. He was very friendly with Benton, and was trying to get him to take a position in his cabinet, which the latter refused, preferring service in the Senate; but now he listened with scant courtesy to the warning, and paid no heed to it. Benton, an intensely proud man, would not speak again; and everything went on as before. The law distributing the surplus among the states began to take effect; under its operations drafts for millions of dollars were made on the banks containing the deposits, and these banks, already sinking, were utterly unable to honor them. It would have been impossible, under any circumstances, for the president to ward off the blow, but he might at least, by a little forethought and preparation, have saved the government from some galling humiliations. Had Benton's advice been followed, the moneys called for by the appropriation acts might have been drawn from the banks, and the disbursing officers might have been prevented from depositing in them the sums which they drew from the treasury to provide for their ordinary expenses; thus the government would have been spared the disgrace of being obliged to stop the actual daily payments to the public servants; and the nation would not have seen such a spectacle as its rulers presented when they had not a dollar with which to pay even a day laborer, while at the same time a law was standing on the statute-book providing for the distribution of forty millions of nominal surplus.

No effort was made to stave off even so much of the impending disaster as was at that late date preventable; and a few days after Van Buren's inauguration the country was in the throes of the worst and most widespread financial panic it has ever seen. The distress was fairly appalling both in its intensity and in its universal distribution. All the banks stopped payment, and bankruptcy was universal. Bank paper depreciated with frightful rapidity, especially in the West; specie increased in value so that all the coin in the country, down to the lowest denomination, was almost immediately taken out of circulation, being either hoarded, or gathered for shipment abroad as bullion. For small change every kind of device was made use of,—tokens, bank-bills for a few cents each, or brass and iron counters.

Benton and others pretended to believe that the panic was the result of a deep-laid plot on the part of the rich classes, who controlled the banks, to excite popular hostility against the Jacksonian Democracy, on account of the caste antagonism which these same richer classes were supposed to feel towards the much-vaunted "party of the people;" and as Benton's mental vision was singularly warped in regard to some subjects, it is possible that the belief was not altogether a pretense. It is entirely unnecessary now seriously to discuss the proposition that it would be possible to drag the commercial classes into so widespread and profoundly secret a conspiracy, with such a vague end in view, and with the certainty that they themselves would be, from a business stand-point, the main sufferers.

The efforts made by Benton and the other Jacksonians to stem the tide of public feeling and direct it through the well-worn channel of suspicious fear of, and anger at, the banks, as the true authors of the general wretchedness, were unavailing; the stream swelled into a torrent and ran like a mill-race in the opposite way. The popular clamor against the administration was deafening; and if much of it was based on good grounds, much of it was also unreasonable. But a very few years before the Jacksonians had appealed to a senseless public dislike of the so-called "money power," in order to help themselves to victory; and now they had the chagrin of seeing an only less irrational outcry raised against themselves in turn, and used to oust them from their places, with the same effectiveness which had previously attended their own frothy and loud-mouthed declamations. The people were more than ready to listen to any one who could point out, or pretend to point out, the authors of, and the reasons for, the calamities that had befallen them. Their condition was pitiable; and this was especially true in the newer and Western states, where in many places there was absolutely no money at all in circulation, even the men of means not being able to get enough coin or its equivalent to make the most ordinary purchases. Trade was at a complete stand-still; laborers were thrown out of employment and left almost starving; farmers, merchants, mechanics, craftsmen of every sort,—all alike were in the direst distress. They naturally, in seeking relief, turned to the government, it being almost always the case that the existing administration receives more credit if the country is prosperous, and greater blame if it is not, than in either case it is rightfully entitled to. The Democracy was now held to strict reckoning, not only for some of its numerous real sins but also for a good many imaginary ones; and the change in the political aspect of many of the commonwealths was astounding. Jackson's own home State of Tennessee became strongly Whig; and Van Buren had the mortification of seeing New York follow suit; two stinging blows to the president and the ex-president. The distress was a godsend to the Whig politicians. They fairly raved in their anger against the administration, and denounced all its acts, good and bad alike, with fluent and incoherent impartiality. Indeed, in their speeches, and in the petitions which they circulated and then sent to the president, they used language that was to the last degree absurd in its violence and exaggeration, and drew descriptions of the iniquities of the rulers of the country which were so overwrought as to be merely ridiculous. The speeches about the panic, and in reference to the proposed laws to alleviate it, were remarkable for their inflation, even in that age of windy oratory.

Van Buren, Benton, and their associates stood bravely up against the storm of indignation which swept over the whole country, and lost neither head nor nerve. They needed both to extricate themselves with any credit from the position in which they were placed. In deference to the urgent wish of almost all the people an extra session of Congress was called especially to deal with the panic. Van Buren's message to this body was a really statesmanlike document, going exhaustively into the subject of the national finances. The Democrats still held the majority in both houses, but there was so large a floating vote, and the margins were so narrow, as to make the administration feel that its hold was precarious.

The first thing to be done was to provide for the immediate wants of the government, which had not enough money to pay even its most necessary running expenses. To make this temporary provision two plans were proposed. The fourth instalment of the surplus—ten millions—was due to the states. As there was really no surplus, but a deficit instead, it was proposed to repeal the deposit law so far as it affected their fourth payment; and treasury notes were to be issued to provide for immediate and pressing needs.

The Whigs frantically attacked the president's proposals, and held him and his party accountable for all the evils of the panic; and in truth it was right enough to hold them so accountable for part; but, after all, the harm was largely due to causes existing throughout the civilized world, and especially to the speculative folly rife among the whole American people. But it is always an easy and a comfortable thing to hold others responsible for what is primarily our own fault.

Benton did not believe, as a matter of principle, in the issue of treasury notes, but supported the bill for that purpose on account of the sore straits the administration was in, and its dire need of assistance from any source. He treated it as a disagreeable but temporary makeshift, only allowable on the ground of the sternest and most grinding necessity, He stated that he supported the issue only because the treasury notes were made out in such a form that they could not become currency; they were merely loan notes. Their chief characteristic was that they bore interest; they were transferable only by indorsement; were payable at a fixed time; were not reissuable, nor of small denominations; and were to be canceled when paid. Such being the case he favored their issue, but expressly stated that he only did so on account of the urgency of the governmental wants; and that he disapproved of any such issue until the ordinary resources of taxes and loans had been tried to the utmost and failed. "I distrust, dislike, and would fain eschew this treasury-note resource; I prefer the direct loans of 1820-21. I could only bring myself to support this present measure when it was urged that there was not time to carry a loan through in its forms; nor even then would I consent to it until every feature of a currency character had been eradicated from the bill."

A sharp struggle took place over the bill brought in by the friends of the administration and advocated by Benton, to repeal the obligation to deposit the fourth instalment of the surplus with the states. This scheme of a distribution, thinly disguised under the name of deposit to soothe the feelings of Calhoun and the other strict constructionist pundits, had worked nothing but mischief from the start; and now that there was no surplus to distribute, it would seem incredible that there should have been opposition to its partial repeal. Yet Webster, Clay, and their followers strenuously opposed even such repeal. It is possible that their motives were honest, but much more probable that they were actuated by partisan hostility to the administration, or that they believed they would increase their own popularity by favoring a plan that seemingly distributed money as a gift among the states. The bill was finally amended so as to make it imperative to pay this fourth instalment in a couple of years; yet it was not then paid, since on the date appointed the national treasury was bankrupt and the states could therefore never get the money,—which was the only satisfactory incident in the whole proceeding. The financial theories of Jackson and Benton were crude and vicious, it is true, but Webster, Clay, and most other public men of the day seem to have held ideas on the subject that were almost, if not quite, as mischievous.

The great financial measures advocated by the administration of Van Buren, and championed with especial zeal by Benton, were those providing for an independent treasury and for hard-money payments; that is, providing that the government should receive nothing but gold and silver for its revenues, and that this gold and silver should be kept by its own officers in real, not constructive, treasuries,—in strong buildings, with special officers to hold the keys. The treasury was to be at Washington, with branches or sub-treasuries at the principal points of collection and disbursement.

These measures, if successful, meant that there would be a total separation of the federal government from all banks; in the political language of the times they became known as those for the divorce of bank and state. Hitherto the local banks chosen by Jackson to receive the deposits had been actively hostile to Biddle's great bank and to its friends; but self-interest now united them all in violent opposition to the new scheme. Webster, Clay, and the Whigs generally fought it bitterly in the Senate; but Calhoun now left his recent allies and joined with Benton in securing its passage. However, it was for the time being defeated in the House of Representatives. Most of the opposition to it was characterized by sheer loud-mouthed demagogy—cries that the government was too aristocratic to accept the money that was thought good enough for the people, and similar claptrap. Benton made a very earnest plea for hard money, and especially denounced the doctrine that it was the government's duty to interfere in any way in private business; for, as usual in times of general distress, a good many people had a vague idea that in some way the government ought to step in and relieve them from the consequences of their own folly.

Meanwhile the banks had been endeavoring to resume specie payment. Those of New York had taken steps in that direction but little more than three months after the suspension. Their weaker Western neighbors, however, were not yet in condition to follow suit; and the great bank at Philadelphia also at first refused to come in with them. But the New York banks persisted in their purpose, resumed payment a year after they had suspended, and eventually the others had to fall into line; the reluctance to do so being of course attributed by Benton to "the factious and wicked machinations" of a "powerful combined political and moneyed confederation"—a shadowy and spectral creation of vivid Jacksonian imaginations, in the existence of which he persisted in believing.

Clay, always active as the friend of the banks, introduced a resolution, nominally to quicken the approach of resumption, but really to help out precisely those weak banks which did not deserve help, making the notes of the resuming banks receivable in payment of all dues to the federal government. This was offered after the banks of New York had resumed, and when all the other solvent banks were on the point of resuming also; so its nominal purpose was already accomplished, as Benton, in a caustic speech, pointed out. He then tore the resolution to shreds, showing that it would be of especial benefit to the insolvent and unsound banks, and would insure a repetition of the worst evils under which the country was already suffering. He made it clear that the proposition practically was to force the government to receive paper promises to pay from banks that were certain to fail, and therefore to force the government in turn to pay out this worthless paper to its honest creditors. Benton's speech was an excellent one, and Clay's resolution was defeated.

All through this bank controversy, and the other controversies relating to it, Benton took the leading part, as mouthpiece of the administration. He heartily supported the suggestion of the president, that a stringent bankrupt law against the banks should be passed. Webster stood out as the principal opponent of this measure, basing his objections mainly upon constitutional grounds; that is, questioning the right, rather than the expediency, of the proposed remedy. Benton answered him at length in a speech showing an immense amount of careful and painstaking study and a wide range of historical reading and legal knowledge; he replied point by point, and more than held his own with his great antagonist. His speech was an exhaustive study of the history and scope of bankruptcy laws against corporations. Benton's capacity for work was at all times immense; he delighted in it for its own sake, and took a most justifiable pride in his wide reading, and especially in his full acquaintance with history, both ancient and modern. He was very fond of illustrating his speeches on American affairs with continual allusions and references to events in foreign countries or in old times, which he considered to be more or less parallel to those he was discussing; and indeed he often dragged in these comparisons when there was no particular need for such a display of his knowledge. He could fairly be called a learned man, for he had studied very many subjects deeply and thoroughly; and though he was too self-conscious and pompous in his utterances not to incur more than the suspicion of pedantry, yet the fact remains that hardly any other man has ever sat in the Senate whose range of information was as wide as his.

He made another powerful and carefully wrought speech in favor of what he called the act to provide for the divorce of bank and state. This bill, as finally drawn, consisted of two distinct parts, one portion making provision for the keeping of the public moneys in an independent treasury, and the other for the hard-money currency, which was all that the government was to accept in payment of revenue dues. This last provision, however, was struck out, and the bill thereby lost the support of Calhoun, who, with Webster, Clay, and the other Whigs, voted against it; but, mainly through Benton's efforts, it passed the Senate, although by a very slender majority. Benton, in his speech, dwelt with especial admiration on the working of the monetary system of France, and held it up as well worthy to be copied by us. Most of the points he made were certainly good ones, although he overestimated the beneficent results that would spring from the adoption of the proposed system, believing that it would put an end for the future to all panics and commercial convulsions. In reality it would have removed only one of the many causes which go to produce the latter, leaving the others free to work as before; the people at large, not the government, were mainly to blame, and even with them it was in some respects their misfortune as much as their fault. Benton's error, however, was natural; like most other men he was unable fully to realize that hardly any phenomenon, even the most simple, can be said to spring from one cause only, and not from a complex and interwoven tissue of causation—and a panic is one of the least simple and most complex of mercantile phenomena. Benton's deep-rooted distrust of and hostility to such banking as then existed in the United States certainly had good grounds for existence.

This distrust was shown again when the bill for the re-charter of the district banks came up. The specie basis of many of them had been allowed to become altogether too low; and Benton showed himself more keenly alive than any other public man to the danger of such a state of things, and argued strongly that a basis of specie amounting to one third the total of liabilities was the only safe proportion, and should be enforced by law. He made a most forcible argument, using numerous and apt illustrations to show the need of his amendment.

Nor was the tireless Missouri senator satisfied even yet; for he introduced a resolution asking leave to bring in a bill to tax the circulation of banks and bankers, and of all corporations, companies, or individuals, issuing paper currency. One object of the bill was to raise revenue; but even more he aimed at the regulation of the currency by the suppression of small notes; and for this end the tax was proposed to be made heaviest on notes under twenty dollars, and to be annually augmented until it had accomplished its object and they had been driven out of circulation. In advocating his measure he used, as was perhaps unavoidable, some arguments that savored strongly of demagogy; but on the whole he made a strong appeal, using as precedents for the law he wished to see enacted both the then existing banking laws in England and those that had obtained previously in the history of the United States.

Taken altogether, while the Jacksonians, during the period of Van Buren's presidency, rightly suffered for their previous financial misdeeds, yet so far as their actions at the time were concerned, they showed to greater advantage than the Whigs. Nor did they waver in their purpose even when the tide of popular feeling changed. The great financial measure of the administration, in which Benton was most interested, the independent treasury bill, he succeeded in getting through the Senate twice; the first time it was lost in the House of Representatives; but on the second occasion, towards the close of Van Buren's term, firmness and perseverance met their reward. The bill passed the Senate by an increased majority, scraped through the House after a bitter contest, and became a law. It developed the system known as that of the sub-Treasury, which has proved satisfactory to the present day.

It was during Van Buren's term that Biddle's great bank, so long the pivot on which turned the fortunes of political parties, finally tottered to its fall. It was ruined by unwise and reckless management; and Benton sang a pæan over its downfall, exulting in its fate as a justification of all that he had said and done. Yet there can be little doubt that its mismanagement became gross only after all connection with the national government had ceased; and its end, attributable to causes not originally existent or likely to exist, can hardly be rightly considered in passing judgment upon the actions of the Jacksonians in reference to it.

CHAPTER X.

LAST DAYS OF THE JACKSONIAN DEMOCRACY.

The difficulty and duration of a war with an Indian tribe depend less upon the numbers of the tribe itself than upon the nature of the ground it inhabits. The two Indian tribes that have caused the most irritating and prolonged struggle are the Apaches, who live in the vast, waterless, mountainous deserts of Arizona and New Mexico, and whom we are at this present moment engaged in subduing, and the Seminoles, who, from among the impenetrable swamps of Florida, bade the whole United States army defiance for seven long years; and this although neither Seminoles nor Apaches ever brought much force into the field, nor inflicted such defeats upon us as have other Indian tribes, like the Creeks and Sioux.

The conflict with the Seminoles was one of the legacies left by Jackson to Van Buren; it lasted as long as the Revolutionary War, cost thirty millions of dollars, and baffled the efforts of several generals and numerous troops, who had previously shown themselves equal to any in the world. The expense, length, and ill-success of the struggle, and a strong feeling that the Seminoles had been wronged, made it a great handle for attack on the administration; and the defense was taken up by Benton, who always accepted completely the Western estimate of any form of the Indian question.

As is usually the case in Indian wars there had been much wrong done by each side; but in this instance we were the more to blame, although the Indians themselves were far from being merely harmless and suffering innocents. The Seminoles were being deprived of their lands in pursuance of the general policy of removing all the Indians west of the Mississippi. They had agreed to go, under pressure, and influenced, probably, by fraudulent representations; but they declined to fulfill their agreement. If they had been treated wisely and firmly they might probably have been allowed to remain without serious injury to the surrounding whites. But no such treatment was attempted, and as a result we were plunged in one of the most harassing Indian wars we ever waged. In their gloomy, tangled swamps, and among the unknown and untrodden recesses of the everglades the Indians found a secure asylum; and they issued from their haunts to burn and ravage almost all the settled part of Florida, fairly depopulating five counties; while the soldiers could rarely overtake them, and when they did, were placed at such a disadvantage that the Indians repulsed or cut off detachment after detachment, generally making a merciless and complete slaughter of each. The great Seminole leader, Osceola, was captured only by deliberate treachery and breach of faith on our part, and the Indians were worn out rather than conquered. This was partly owing to their remarkable capacities as bush-fighters, but infinitely more to the nature of their territory.

Our troops generally fought with great bravery; but there is very little else in the struggle, either as regards its origin or the manner in which it was carried on, to which an American can look back with any satisfaction. We usually group all our Indian wars together, in speaking of their justice or injustice; and thereby show flagrant ignorance. The Sioux and Cheyennes, for instance, have more often been sinning than sinned against; for example, the so-called Chivington or Sandy Creek Massacre, in spite of certain most objectionable details, was on the whole as righteous and beneficial a deed as ever took place on the frontier. On the other hand, the most cruel wrongs have been perpetrated by whites upon perfectly peaceable and unoffending tribes like those of California, or the Nez Perçés. Yet the emasculated professional humanitarians mourn as much over one set of Indians as over the other—and indeed, on all points connected with Indian management, are as untrustworthy and unsafe leaders as would be an equal number of the most brutal white borderers. But the Seminole War was one of those where the Eastern, or humanitarian view was more nearly correct than was any other; although even here the case was far from being entirely one-sided.

Benton made an elaborate but not always candid defense of the administration, both as to the origin and as to the prosecution of the war. He attempted to show that the Seminoles had agreed to go West, had broken their treaty without any reason, had perpetrated causeless massacres, had followed up their successes with merciless butcheries, which last statement was true; and that Osceola had forfeited all claim or right to have a flag of truce protect him. There was a certain justice in his position even on these questions, and when he came to defend the conduct of our soldiers he had the right entirely with him. They were led by the same commander, and belonged to the same regiments, that in Canada had shown themselves equal to the famous British infantry; they had to contend with the country, rather than with their enemies, as the sweltering heat, the stagnant lagoons, the quaking morasses, and the dense forests of Florida made it almost impossible for an army to carry on a successful campaign. Moreover, the Seminoles were well armed; and many tribes of North American Indians show themselves, when with good weapons and on their own ground, more dangerous antagonists than would be an equal number of the best European troops. Indeed, under such conditions they can only be contended with on equal terms if the opposing white force is made up of frontiersmen who are as good woodsmen and riflemen as themselves, and who, moreover, have been drilled by some man like Jackson, who knows how to handle them to the best advantage, both in disciplining their lawless courage and in forcing them to act under orders and together,—the lack of which discipline and power of supporting each other has often rendered an assemblage of formidable individual border-fighters a mere disorderly mob when brought into the field.

The war dragged on tediously. The troops—regulars, volunteers, and militia alike—fought the Indians again and again; there were pitched battles, surprises, ambuscades, and assaults on places of unknown strength; hundreds of soldiers were slain in battle or by treachery, hundreds of settlers were slaughtered in their homes, or as they fled from them; the bloody Indian forays reached even to the outskirts of Tallahatchee and to within sight of the walls of quaint old St. Augustine. Little by little, however, the power of the Seminoles was broken; their war bands were scattered and driven from the field, hundreds of their number were slain in fight, and five times as many surrendered and were taken west of the Mississippi. The white troops marched through Florida down to and into the everglades, and crossed it backwards and forwards, from the Gulf of Mexico to the Atlantic Ocean; they hunted their foes from morass to morass and from hummock to hummock; they mapped out the whole hitherto unknown country; they established numerous posts; opened hundreds of miles of wagon road; and built very many causeways and bridges. But they could not end the war. The bands of Indians broke up and entirely ceased to offer resistance to bodies of armed whites; but as individuals they continued as dangerous to the settlers as ever, prowling out at night like wild beasts from their fastnesses in the dark and fetid swamps, murdering, burning, and ravaging in all the outlying settlements, and destroying every lonely farm-house or homestead.

There was but one way in which the war could be finally ended, and that was to have the territory occupied by armed settlers; in other words, to have it won and held exactly as almost all the land of the United States has been in the beginning. Benton introduced a bill to bring this about, giving to every such settler a good inheritance in the soil as a reward for his enterprise, toil, and danger; and the war was finished only by the adoption of this method. He supported his bill in a very effective speech, showing that the proposed way was the only one by which a permanent conquest could be effected; he himself had, when young, seen it put into execution in Tennessee and Kentucky, where the armed settlers, with their homesteads in the soil, formed the vanguard of the white advance: where the rifle-bearing backwoodsmen went forth to fight and to cultivate, living in assemblages of block-houses at first and separating into individual settlements afterwards. The work had to be done with axe, spade, and rifle alike. Benton rightly insisted that there was no longer need of a large army in Florida:—

> Why, the men who are there now can find nobody to fight!
> It is two years since a fight has been had. Ten men who will
> avoid surprises and ambuscades can now go from one end
> of Florida to the other. As warriors, these Indians no longer

appear; it is only as assassins, as robbers, as incendiaries, that they lurk about. What is now wanted is not an army to fight, but settlers and cultivators to take possession and keep possession; and the armed cultivator is the man for that. The block-house is the first house to be built in an Indian country; the stockade the first fence to be put up. Within that block-house, or within a hollow square of block-houses, two miles long on each side, two hundred yards apart, and inclosing a good field, safe habitations are to be found for families. Cultivation and defense then go hand in hand. The heart of the Indian sickens when he hears the crowing of the cock, the barking of the dog, the sound of the axe, and the crack of the rifle. These are the true evidences of the dominion of the white man; these are the proofs that the owner has come and means to stay, and then the Indians feel it to be time for them to go. While soldiers alone are in the country they feel their presence to be temporary; that they are mere sojourners in the land, and sooner or later must go away. It is the settler alone, the armed settler, whose presence announces the dominion, the permanent dominion, of the white man.

Benton's ideas were right, and were acted upon. It is impossible even to subdue an Indian tribe by the army alone; the latter can only pave the way for and partially protect the armed settlers who are to hold the soil.

Benton continued to take a great interest in the disposal of the public lands, as was natural in a senator from the West, where the bulk of these lands lay. He was always a great advocate of a homestead law. During Van Buren's administration, he succeeded in getting two or three bills on the subject through the Senate. One of these allowed lands that had been five years in the market to be reduced in price to a dollar an acre, and if they stood five years longer to go down to seventy-five cents. The bill was greatly to the interest of the Western farmer in the newer, although not necessarily the newest, parts of the country. The man who went on the newest land was in turn provided for by the preëmption bill, which secured the privilege of first purchase to the actual settler on any lands to which the Indian title had been extinguished; to be paid for at the minimum price of public lands at the time. An effort was made to confine the benefits of this proposed law to citizens of the United States, excluding unnaturalized foreigners from its action. Benton, as representing the new states, who desired immigrants of every kind, whether foreign or native, successfully opposed this. He pointed out that there was no question of conferring political rights, which involved the management of the government, and which should not be conferred until the foreigner had become a naturalized citizen; it was merely a question of allowing the alien a right to maintain himself and to support his family. He especially opposed the amendment on account of the class of foreigners it would affect. Aliens who wished to take up public lands were not paupers or criminals, and did not belong to the shiftless and squalid foreign mob that drifted into the great cities of the sea-board and the interior; but on the contrary were among our most enterprising, hardy, and thrifty citizens, who had struck out for themselves into the remote parts of the new states and had there begun to bring the wilderness into subjection. Such men deserved to be encouraged in every way, and should receive from the preëmption laws the same benefits that would enure to native-born citizens. The third bill introduced, which passed the Senate but failed in the House, was one to permit the public lands sold to be immediately taxed by the states in which they lay. Originally these lands had been sold upon credit, the total amount not being paid, nor the title passed, until five years after the sale; and during this time it would have been unjust to tax them, as failure in paying the installments to the government would have let the lands revert to the latter; but when the cash system was substituted for credit Benton believed that there was no longer reason why the new lands should not bear their share of the state burdens.

During Van Buren's administration the standard of public honesty, which had been lowering with frightful rapidity ever since, with Adams, the men of high moral tone had gone out of power, went almost as far down as it could go; although things certainly did not change for the better under Tyler and Polk. Not only was there the most impudent and unblushing rascality among the public servants of the nation, but the people themselves, through their representatives in the state legislatures, went to work to swindle their honest creditors. Many states, in the rage for public improvements, had contracted debts which they now refused to pay; in many cases they were unable, or at least so professed themselves, even to pay the annual interest. The debts of the states were largely held abroad; they had been converted into stock and held in shares, which had gone into a great number of hands, and now, of course, became greatly depreciated in value. It is a painful and shameful page in our history; and every man connected with the repudiation of the states' debts ought, if remembered at all, to be remembered only with scorn and contempt. However, time has gradually shrouded from our sight both the names of the leaders in the repudiation and the names of the victims whom they swindled. Two alone, one in each class, will always be kept in mind. Before Jefferson Davis took his place among the arch-traitors in our annals he had already long been known as one of the chief repudiators; it was not unnatural that to dishonesty towards the creditors of the public he should afterwards add treachery towards the public itself. The one most prominent victim was described by Benton himself: "The Reverend Sydney Smith, of witty memory, but amiable withal, was accustomed to lose all his amiability, but no part of his wit, when he spoke of his Pennsylvania bonds—which, in fact, was very often."

Many of the bond-holders, however, did not manifest their grief by caustic wit, but looked to more substantial relief; and did their best to bring about the assumption of the state debts, in some form, whether open or disguised, by the federal government. The British capitalists united with many American capitalists to work for some such action; and there were plenty of people in the states willing enough to see it done. Of course it would have been criminal folly on the part of the federal government to take any such step; and Benton determined to meet and check the effort at the very beginning. The London Bankers' Circular had contained a proposition recommending that the Congress of the United States should guarantee, or otherwise provide for, the ultimate payment of the debts which the states had contracted for state or local purposes. Benton introduced a series of resolutions declaring utter opposition to the proposal, both on the ground of expediency and on that of constitutionality. The resolutions were perfectly proper in their purpose, but were disfigured by that cheap species of demagogy which consists in denouncing purely supposititious foreign interference, complicated by an allusion to Benton's especial pet terror, the inevitable money power. As he put it: "Foreign interference and influence are far more dangerous in the invidious intervention of the moneyed power than in the forcible invasions of fleets and armies."

An attempt was made directly to reverse the effect of the resolutions by amending them so as to provide that the public land revenue should be divided among the states, to help them in the payment of these debts. Both Webster and Clay supported this amendment, but it was fortunately beaten by a large vote.

Benton's speech, like the resolutions in support of which he spoke, was right in its purpose, but contained much matter that was beside the mark. He had worked himself into such a condition over the supposititious intrigues of the "money power"—an attack on which is almost always sure to be popular— that he was very certain to discover evidence of their existence on all, even the most unlikely, occasions; and it is difficult to think that he was not himself aware how overdrawn was his prophecy of the probable interference of foreign powers in our affairs, if the resolutions he had presented were not adopted.

The tariff had once more begun to give trouble, and the South was again complaining of its workings, aware that she was falling always more to the rear in the race for prosperity, and blindly attributing her failure to everything but the true reason,—the existence of slavery. Even Benton himself showed a curiously pathetic eagerness to prove both to others and himself that the cause of the increasing disparity in growth, and incompatibility in interest between the two sections, must be due to some temporary and artificial cause, and endeavored to hide from all eyes, even from his own, the fact that the existence of slavery was working, slowly but surely, and with steadily increasing rapidity, to rend in sunder the Union which he loved and served with such heartfelt devotion. He tried to prove that the main cause of discontent was to be found in the tariff and other laws, which favored the North at the expense of the South. At the same time he entered an eloquent plea for a warmer feeling between the sections, and pointed out the absolute hopelessness of attempting to better the situation in any way by disunion. The great Missourian could look back with fond pride and regret to the condition of the South as it was during and immediately after the colonial days, when it was the seat of wealth, power, high living, and free-handed hospitality, and was filled to overflowing with the abounding life of its eager and turbulent sons. The change for the worse in its relative condition was real and great. He reproved his fellow-Southerners for attributing this change to a single cause, the unequal working of the federal government, "which gave all the benefits of the Union to the South and all its burdens to the North;" he claimed that it was due to many other causes as well. Yet those whom he rebuked were as near right as he was; for the change *was* due in the main to only one cause—but that cause was slavery. It is almost pitiful to see the strong, stern, self-reliant statesman refusing, with nervous and passionate willfulness, to look the danger in the face, and, instead thereof, trying to persuade himself into the belief that "the remedy lies in the right working of the Constitution; in the cessation of unequal legislation; in the reduction of the inordinate expenses of the government; in its return to the simple, limited, and economical machine it was intended to be; and in the revival of fraternal feelings and respect for each other's rights and just complaints." Like many another man he thought, or tried to think, that by sweeping the dust from the door-sill he could somehow stave off the whirling rush of the sand-storm.

The compromise tariff of 1833 had abolished all specific duties, establishing *ad valorem* ones in their place; and the result had been great uncertainty and injustice in its working. Now whether a protective tariff is right or wrong may be open to question; but if it exists at all, it should work as simply and with as much certainty and exactitude as possible; if its interpretation varies, or if it is continually meddled with by Congress, great damage ensues. It is in reality of far less importance that a law should be ideally right than that it should be certain and steady in its workings. Even supposing that a high tariff is all wrong, it would work infinitely better for the country than would a series of changes between high and low duties. Benton strongly advocated a return to specific duties, as being simpler, surer, and better on every account. In commenting on the *ad valorem* duties, he showed how they had been adopted blindly and without discussion by the frightened, silent multitude of congressmen and senators, who jumped at Clay's compromise bill in 1833 as giving them a loop-hole of escape from a situation where they would have had to face evil consequences, no matter what stand they took. Benton's comment on men of this stamp deserves chronicling, from its justice and biting severity: "It (the compromise act) was passed by the aid of the votes of those—always a considerable *per centum* in every public body—to whom the name of compromise is an irresistible attraction; amiable men, who would do no wrong of themselves, and without whom the designing could also do but little wrong."

He not only devoted himself to the general subject of the tariff in relation to specific duties, but he also took up several prominent abuses. One subject, on which he was never tired of harping with monotonous persistency, was the duty on salt. The idea of making salt free had become one which he was almost as fond of bringing into every discussion, no matter how inappropiate to the matter in hand, as he was of making irrelevant and abusive allusions to his much-enduring and long-suffering hobby, the iniquitous "money power." Benton had all the tenacity of a snapping turtle, and was as firm a believer in the policy of "continuous hammering" as Grant himself. His tenacity and his pertinacious refusal to abandon any contest, no matter what the odds were against him, and no matter how often he had to return to the charge, formed two of his most invaluable qualities, and when called into play on behalf of such an object as the preservation of the Union, cannot receive too high praise at our hands; for they did the country services so great and lasting that they should never be forgotten. It would have been fortunate indeed if Clay and Webster had possessed the fearless, aggressive courage and iron will of the rugged Missourian, who was so often pitted against them in the political arena. But when Benton's attention was firmly fixed on the accomplishment of something comparatively trivial, his dogged, stubborn, and unyielding earnestness drew him into making efforts of which the disproportion to the result aimed at was rather droll. Nothing could thwart him or turn him aside; and though slow to take up an idea, yet, if it was once in his head, to drive it out was a simply hopeless task. These qualities were of such invaluable use to the state on so many great occasions that we can well afford to treat them merely with a good-humored laugh, when we see them exercised on behalf of such a piece of foolishness as, for example, the expunging resolution.

The repeal of the salt tax, then, was a particular favorite in Benton's rather numerous stable of hobbies, because it gave free scope for the use of sentimental as well as of economic arguments. He had the right of the question, and was not in the least daunted by his numerous rebuffs and the unvarying ill success of his efforts. Speaking in 1840, he stated that he had been urging the repeal for twelve years; and for the purpose of furnishing data with which to compare such a period of time, and without the least suspicion that there was anything out of the way in the comparison, he added, in a solemn parenthesis, that this was two years longer than the siege of Troy lasted. In the same speech was a still choicer morsel of eloquence about salt: "The Supreme Ruler of the Universe has done everything to supply his creatures with it; man, the fleeting shadow of an instant, invested with his little brief authority, has done much to deprive them of it." After which he went on to show a really extensive acquaintance with the history of salt taxes and monopolies, and with the uses and physical structure and surroundings of the mineral itself—all which might have taught his hearers that a man may combine much erudition with a total lack of the sense of humor. The salt tax is dragged, neck and heels, into many of Benton's speeches much as Cooper manages, on all possible occasions, throughout his novels, to show the unlikeness of the Bay of Naples to the Bay of New York—not the only point of resemblance, by the way, between the characters of the Missouri statesman and the New York novelist. Whether the subject under discussion was the taxation of bank-notes, or the abolition of slavery, made very little difference to Benton as to introducing an allusion to the salt monopoly. One of his happy arguments in favor of the repeal, which was addressed to an exceedingly practical and commonplace Congress, was that the early Christian disciples had been known as the salt of the earth—a biblical metaphor, which Benton kindly assured his hearers was very expressive; and added that a salt tax was morally as well as politically wrong, and in fact "was a species of impiety."

But in attacking some of the abuses which had developed out of the tariff of 1833 Benton made a very shrewd and practical speech, without permitting himself to indulge in any such intellectual pranks as accompanied his salt orations. He especially aimed at reducing the drawbacks on sugar, molasses, and one or two other articles. In accordance with our whole clumsy, hap-hazard system of dealing with the tariff we had originally put very high duties on the articles in question, and then had allowed correspondingly heavy drawbacks; and yet, when in 1833, by Clay's famous compromise tariff bill, the duties were reduced to a fractional part of what they had previously been, no parallel reduction was made in the drawbacks, although Benton (supported by Webster) made a vain effort even then, while the compromise bill was on its passage, to have the injustice remedied. As a consequence, the exporters of sugar and rum, instead of drawing back the exact amounts paid into the treasury, drew back several times as much; and the ridiculous result was that certain exporters were paid a naked bounty out of the treasury, and received pay for doing and suffering nothing. In 1839 the drawback paid on the exportation of refined sugar exceeded the amount of revenue derived from imported sugar by over twenty thousand dollars. Benton showed this clearly, by unimpeachable statistics, and went on to prove that in that year the whole amount of the revenue from brown and clayed sugar, plus the above-mentioned twenty thousand dollars, was paid over to twenty-nine sugar refiners; and that these men thus "drew back" from the treasury what they had never put into it. Abuses equally gross existed in relation to various other articles. But in spite of the clear justice of his case Benton was able at first to make but little impression on Congress; and it was some time before matters were straightened out, as all the protective interests felt obliged to make common cause with each other, no matter what evils might be perpetrated by their taking such action.

Towards the close of Van Buren's administration, when he was being assailed on every side, as well for what Jackson as for what he himself had done or left undone, one of the chief accusations brought against him was that he had squandered the public money, and that, since Adams had been ousted from the presidency, the expenses of running the government had increased out of all proportion to what was proper. There was good ground for their complaint, as the waste and peculation in some of the departments had been very great; but Benton, in an elaborate defense of both Jackson and Van Buren, succeeded in showing that at least certain of the accusations were unfounded—although he had to stretch a point or two in trying to make good his claim that the administration was really economical, being reduced to the rather lame expedient of ruling out about two thirds of the expenditures on the ground that they were "extraordinary."

The charge of extravagance was one of the least of the charges urged against the Jacksonian Democrats during the last days of their rule. While they had been in power the character of the public service had deteriorated frightfully, both as regarded its efficiency and infinitely more as regarded its honesty; and under Van Buren the amount of money stolen by the public officers, compared to the amount handed in to the treasury, was greater than ever before or since. For this the Jacksonians were solely and absolutely responsible; they drove out the merit system of making appointments, and introduced the "spoils" system in its place; and under the latter they chose a peculiarly dishonest and incapable set of officers, whose sole recommendation was to be found in the knavish trickery and low cunning that enabled them to manage the ignorant voters who formed the backbone of Jackson's party. The statesmen of the Democracy in after days forgot the good deeds of the Jacksonians; they lost their attachment to the Union, and abandoned their championship of hard money; but they never ceased to cling to the worst legacy their predecessors had left them. The engrafting of the "spoils" system on our government was, of all the results of Jacksonian rule, the one which was most permanent in its effects.

All these causes—the corruption of the public officials, the extravagance of the government, and the widespread distress, which might be regarded as the aftermath of its ruinous financial policy—combined with others that were as little to the discredit of the Jacksonians as they were to the credit of the Whigs, brought about the overthrow of the former. There was much poetic justice in the fact that the presidential election which decided their fate was conducted on as purely irrational principles, and was as merely one of sound and fury, as had been the case in the election twelve years previously, when they came into power. The Whigs, having exhausted their language in denouncing their opponents for nominating a man like Andrew Jackson, proceeded to look about in their own party to find one who should come as near him as possible in all the attributes that had given him so deep a hold on the people; and they succeeded perfectly when they pitched on the old Indian fighter, Harrison. "Tippecanoe" proved quite as effective a war-cry in bringing about the downfall of the Jacksonians as "Old Hickory" had shown itself to be a dozen years previously in raising them up. General Harrison had already shown himself to be a good soldier, and a loyal and honest public servant, although by no means standing in the first rank either as regards war-craft or state-craft; but the mass of his supporters apparently considered the facts, or supposed facts, that he lived in a log-cabin the walls of which were decorated with coon-skins, and that he drank hard cider from a gourd, as being more important than his capacity as a statesman or his past services to the nation.

The Whigs having thus taken a shaft from the Jacksonians' quiver, it was rather amusing to see the latter, in their turn, hold up their hands in horror at the iniquity of what would now be called a "hurrah" canvass; blandly ignoring the fact that it was simply a copy of their own successful proceedings. Says Benton, with amusing gravity: "The class of inducements addressed to the passions and imaginations of the people was such as history blushes to record," a remark that provokes criticism, when it is remembered that Benton had been himself a prominent actor on the Jacksonian side in the campaigns of '28 and '32, when it was exclusively to "the passions and imaginations of the people" that all arguments were addressed.

The Democrats did not long remain out of power; and they kept the control of the governmental policy in their hands pretty steadily until the time of the civil war; nevertheless it is true that with the defeat of Van Buren the Jacksonian Democracy, as such, lost forever its grip on the direction of national affairs. When, under Polk, the Democrats came back, they came under the lead of the very men whom the original Jacksonians had opposed and kept down. With all their faults, Jackson and Benton were strong Union men, and under them their party was a Union party. Calhoun and South Carolina, and the disunionists in the other Southern States were their bitter foes. But the disunion and extreme slavery elements within the Democratic ranks were increasing rapidly all the time; and they had obtained complete and final control when the party reappeared as victors after their defeat in 1840. Until Van Buren's overthrow the nationalists had held the upper hand in shaping Democratic policy; but after that event the leadership of the party passed completely into the hands of the separatists.

The defeat of Van Buren marks an era in more ways than one. During his administration slavery played a less prominent part in politics than did many other matters; this was never so again. His administration was the last in which this question, or the question springing from it, did not overtop and dwarf in importance all others. Again, the presidential election of 1840 was the last into which slavery did not enter as a most important, and in fact as the vital and determining factor. In the contest between Van Buren and Harrison it did not have the least influence upon the result. Moreover, Van Buren was the last Democratic president who ruled over a Union of states; all his successors, up to the time of Lincoln's election, merely held sway over a Union of sections. The spirit of separation had identified itself with the maintenance of slavery, and the South was rapidly uniting into a compact array of states with interests that were hostile to the North on the point most vitally affecting the welfare of the whole country.

No great question involving the existence of slavery was brought before the attention of Congress during Van Buren's term of office; nor was the matter mooted except in the eternal wrangles over receiving the abolitionist petitions. Benton kept silent in these discussions, although voting to receive the petitions. As he grew older he continually grew wiser, and better able to do good legislative work on all subjects; but he was not yet able to realize that the slavery question was one which could not be kept down, and which was bound to force itself into the sphere of national politics. He still insisted that it was only dragged before Congress by a few fanatics at the North, and that in the South it was made the instrument by which designing and unscrupulous men wished to break up the federal republic. His devotion to the Union, ever with him the chief and overmastering thought, made him regard with horror and aversion any man, at the North or at the South, who brought forward a question so fraught with peril to its continuance. He kept trying to delude himself into the belief that the discussion and the danger would alike gradually die away, and the former state of peaceful harmony between the sections, and freedom from disunion excitement, would return.

But the time for such an ending already lay in the past; thereafter the outlook was to grow steadily darker year by year. Slavery lowered like a thunder-storm on the horizon; and though sometimes it might seem for a moment to break away, yet in reality it had reached that stage when, until the final all-engulfing outburst took place, the clouds were bound for evermore to return after the rain.

CHAPTER XI.

THE PRESIDENT WITHOUT A PARTY.

The Whigs in 1840 completely overthrew the Democrats, and for the first time elected a president and held the majority in both houses of Congress. Yet, as it turned out, all that they really accomplished was to elect a president without a party, for Harrison died when he had hardly more than sat in the presidential chair, and was succeeded by the vice-president, Tyler of Virginia.

Harrison was a true Whig; he was, when nominated, a prominent member of the Whig party, although of course not to be compared with its great leader, Henry Clay, or with its most mighty intellectual chief and champion in the Northeast, Daniel Webster, whose mutual rivalry had done much to make his nomination possible. Tyler, however, could hardly be called a Whig at all; on the contrary, he belonged rightfully in the ranks of those extreme Democrats who were farthest removed from the Whig standard, and who were as much displeased with the Union sentiments of the Jacksonians as they were with the personal tyranny of Jackson himself. He was properly nothing but a dissatisfied Democrat, who hated the Jacksonians, and had been nominated only because the Whig politicians wished to strengthen their ticket and insure its election by bidding for the votes of the discontented in the ranks of their foes. Now a chance stroke of death put the presidency in the hands of one who represented this, the smallest, element in the coalition that overthrew Van Buren.

The principles of the Whigs were hazily outlined at the best, and the party was never a very creditable organization; indeed, throughout its career, it could be most easily defined as the opposition to the Democracy. It was a free constructionist party, believing in giving a liberal interpretation to the doctrines of the Constitution; otherwise, its principles were purely economic, as it favored a high tariff, internal improvements, a bank, and kindred schemes; and its leaders, however they might quarrel among themselves, agreed thoroughly in their devout hatred of Jackson and all his works.

It was on this last point only that Tyler came in. His principles had originally been ultra-Democratic. He had been an extreme strict constructionist, had belonged to that wing of the Democracy which inclined more and more towards separation, and had thus, on several grounds, found himself opposed to Jackson, Benton, and their followers. Indeed, he went into opposition to his original party for reasons akin to those that influenced Calhoun; and Seward's famous remark about the "ill-starred coalition between Whigs and Nullifiers" might with certain changes have been applied to the presidential election of 1840 quite as well as to the senatorial struggles to which it had reference.

Tyler, however, had little else in common with Calhoun, and least of all his intellect. He has been called a mediocre man; but this is unwarranted flattery. He was a politician of monumental littleness. Owing to the nicely-divided condition of parties, and to the sheer accident which threw him into a position of such prominence that it allowed him to hold the balance of power between them, he was enabled to turn politics completely topsy-turvy; but his chief mental and moral attributes were peevishness, fretful obstinacy, inconsistency, incapacity to make up his own mind, and the ability to quibble indefinitely over the most microscopic and hair-splitting plays upon words, together with an inordinate vanity that so blinded him to all outside feeling as to make him really think that he stood a chance to be renominated for the presidency.

The Whigs, especially in the Senate, under Henry Clay, prepared at once to push through various measures that should undo the work of the Jacksonians. Clay was boastfully and domineeringly sure of the necessity of applying to actual governmental work the economic theories that formed the chief stock in trade of his party. But it was precisely on these economic theories that Tyler split off from the Whigs. The result was that very shortly the real leader of the dominant party, backed by almost all his fellow party men in both houses of Congress, was at daggers drawn with the nominal Whig president, who in his turn was supported only by a "corporal's guard" of followers in the House of Representatives, by all the office-holders whom fear of removal reduced to obsequious subserviency, and by a knot of obscure politicians who used him for their own ends, and worked alternately on his vanity and on his fears. The Democrats, led by Benton, played out their own game, and were the only parties to the three-cornered fight who came out of it with profit. The details now offer rather dry reading, as the economic theories of all the contestants were more or less crude, the results of the conflict indecisive, and the effects upon our history ephemeral.

Clay began by a heated revival of one of Jackson's worst ideas, namely, that when the people elect a president they thereby mark with the seal of their approval any and every measure with which that favored mortal or his advisers may consider themselves identified, and indorse all his and their previous actions. He at once declared that the people had shown, by the size of Harrison's majority, that they demanded the repeal of the independent treasury act, and the passage of various other laws in accordance with some of his own favorite hobbies, two out of three voters, as a matter of fact, probably never having given a second thought to any of them. Accordingly he proceeded to introduce a whole batch of bills, which he alleged that it was only yielding due respect to the spirit of Democracy to pass forthwith.

Benton, however, even outdid Clay in paying homage to what he was pleased to call the "democratic idea." At this time he speaks of the last session of the

Twenty-Sixth Congress as being "barren of measures, and necessarily so, as being the last of an administration superseded by the popular voice and soon to expire; and therefore restricted by a sense of propriety, during the brief remainder of its existence, to the details of business and the routine of service." According to this theory an interregnum of some sixteen weeks would intervene between the terms of service of every two presidents. He also speaks of Tyler as having, when the legislature of Virginia disapproved of a course he wished to follow, resigned his seat "in obedience to the democratic principle," which, according to his views, thus completely nullified the section of the Constitution providing for a six years' term of service in the Senate. In truth Benton, like most other Jacksonian and Jeffersonian leaders, became both foolish and illogical when he began to talk of the bundle of vague abstractions, which he knew collectively as the "democratic principle." Although not so bad as many of his school he had yet gradually worked himself up to a belief that it was almost impious to pay anything but servile heed to the "will of the majority;" and was quite unconscious that to surrender one's own manhood and judgment to a belief in the divine right of kings was only one degree more ignoble, and was not a shadow more logical, and but little more defensible, than it was blindly to deify a majority—not of the whole people, but merely of a small fraction consisting of those who happened to be of a certain sex, to have reached a certain age, to belong to a certain race, and to fulfill some other conditions. In fact there is no natural or divine law in the matter at all; how large a portion of the population should be trusted with the control of the government is a question of expediency merely. In any purely native American community manhood suffrage works infinitely better than would any other system of government, and throughout our country at large, in spite of the large number of ignorant foreign-born or colored voters, it is probably preferable as it stands to any modification of it; but there is no more "natural right" why a white man over twenty-one should vote than there is why a negro woman under eighteen should not. "Civil rights" and "personal freedom" are not terms that necessarily imply the right to vote. People make mistakes when governing themselves, exactly as they make mistakes when governing others; all that can be said is, that in the former case their self-interest is on the side of good government, whereas in the latter it always may be, and often must be, the reverse; so that, when any people reaches a certain stage of mental development and of capacity to take care of its own concerns, it is far better that it should itself take the reins. The distinctive features of the American system are its guarantees of personal independence and individual freedom; that is, as far as possible, it guarantees to each man his right to live as he chooses and to regulate his own private affairs as he wishes, without being interfered with or tyrannized over by an individual, or by an oligarchic minority, or by a democratic majority; while, when the interests of the whole community are at stake, it is found best in the long run to let them be managed in accordance with the wishes of the majority of those presumably concerned.

Clay's flourish of trumpets foreboded trouble and disturbance to the Jacksonian camp. At last he stood at the head of a party controlling both branches of the legislative body, and devoted to his behests; and, if a little doubtful about the president, he still believed he could frighten him into doing as he was bid. He had long been in the minority, and had seen his foes ride roughshod over all he most believed in; and now he prepared to pay them back in their own coin and to leave a heavy balance on his side of the reckoning. Nor could any Jacksonian have shown himself more domineering and influenced by a more insolent disregard for the rights of others than Clay did in his hour of triumph. On the other side, Benton braced himself with dogged determination for the struggle; for he was one of those men who fight a losing or a winning battle with equal resolution.

Tyler's first message to Congress read like a pretty good Whig document. It did not display any especial signs of his former strict construction theories, and gave little hope to the Democrats. The leader of the latter, indeed, Benton, commented upon both it and its author with rather grandiloquent severity, on account of its latitudinarian bias, and of its recommendation of a bank of some sort. However, the ink with which the message was written could hardly have been dry before the president's mind began to change. He himself probably had very little idea what he intended to do, and so contrived to give the Whigs the impression that he would act in accordance with their wishes; but the leaven had already begun working in his mind, and, not having much to work on, soon changed it so completely that he was willing practically to eat his own words.

Shortly after Tyler had sent in his message outlining what legislation he deemed proper, he being by virtue of his position the nominal and titular leader of the Whigs, Clay, who was their real and very positive chief, and who was, moreover, determined to assert his chieftainship, in his turn laid down a programme for his party to follow, introducing a series of resolutions declaring it necessary to pass a bill to repeal the sub-treasury act, another to establish a bank, another to distribute the proceeds of the public land sales, and one or two more, to which was afterwards added a bankruptcy measure.

The sub-treasury bill was first taken up and promptly passed and signed. Benton, of course, led the hopeless fight against it, making a long and elaborate speech, insisting that the finances were in excellent shape, as they were, showing the advantages of hard money, and denouncing the bill on account of the extreme suddenness with which it took effect, and because it made no provision for any substitute. He also alluded caustically to the curious and anomalous bank bill, which was then being patched up by the Whig leaders so as to get it into some such shape that the president would sign it.

The other three important measures, that is, the bank, distribution, and bankruptcy bills, were all passed nearly together; as Benton pointed out, they were got through only by a species of bargain and sale, the chief supporters of each agreeing to support the other, so as to get their own pet measure through. "All must go together or fall together. This is the decree out of doors. When the sun dips below the horizon a private congress is held; the fate of the measures is decided; a bundle is tied together; and while one goes ahead as a bait, another is held back as a rod."

The bankruptcy bill went through and was signed. It was urged by all the large debtor class, whose ranks had been filled to overflowing by the years of wild speculation and general bank suspension and insolvency. These debtors were quite numerous enough to constitute an important factor in politics, but Benton disregarded them nevertheless, and fought the bill as stoutly as he did its companions, alleging that it was a gross outrage on honesty and on the rights of property, and was not a bankrupt law at all, but practically an insolvent law for the abolition of debts at the will of the debtor. He pointed out grave and numerous defects of detail, and gave an exhaustive abstract of bankruptcy legislation in general; the speech gave evidence of the tireless industry and wide range of learning for which Benton was preëminently distinguished.

The third bill to be taken up and passed was that providing for the distribution of the public lands revenue, and thus indirectly for assuming the debts of the states. Tyler, in his message, had characteristically stated that, though it would be wholly unconstitutional for the federal government to assume the debts of the states, yet it would be highly proper for it to give the latter money wherewith to pay them. Clay had always been an enthusiastic advocate of a distribution bill; and accordingly one was now passed and signed with the least possible delay. It was an absolutely indefensible measure. The treasury was empty, and loan and tax bills were pending at the very moment, in order to supply money for the actual running of the government. As Benton pointed out, Congress had been called together (a special session having been summoned by Harrison before his death) to raise revenue, and the first thing done was to squander it. The distribution took place when the treasury reports showed a deficit of sixteen millions of dollars. The bill was pushed through mainly by the states which had repudiated their debts in whole or in part; and as these debts were largely owed abroad, many prominent foreign banking-houses and individuals took an active part in lobbying for the bill. Benton was emphatically right in his opposition to the measure, but he was very wrong in some of the grounds he took. Thus he inveighed vigorously against the foreign capitalists who had come to help push the bill through Congress; but he did not have anything to say against the scoundrelly dishonesty displayed by certain states towards their creditors, which had forced these capitalists into the endeavor to protect themselves. He also incidentally condemned the original assumption by the national government of the debts of the states, at the time of the formation of the Constitution, which was an absolute necessity; and his constitutional views throughout seem rather strained. But he was right beyond cavil on the main point. It was criminal folly to give the states the impression that they would be allowed to create debts over which Congress could have no control, yet which Congress in the end would give them the money to pay. To reward a state for repudiating a debt by giving her the wherewithal to pay it was a direct and unequivocal encouragement of dishonesty. In every respect the bill was wholly improper; and Benton's attitude towards it and towards similar schemes was incomparably better than the position of Clay, Webster, and the other Whigs.

Both the bankrupt bill and the distribution bill were repealed very shortly; the latter before it had time to take effect. This was an emphatic indorsement by the public of Benton's views, and a humiliating rebuke to the Whig authors of the measures. Indeed, the whole legislation of the session was almost absolutely fruitless in its results.

One feature of the struggle was an attempt by Clay, promptly and successfully resisted by Benton and Calhoun, to institute the hour limit for speeches in the Senate. There was a good deal of excuse for Clay's motion. The House could cut off debate by the previous question, which the Senate could not, and nevertheless had found it necessary to establish the hour limit in addition. Of course it is highly undesirable that there should not be proper freedom of debate in Congress; but it is quite as hurtful to allow a minority to exercise their privileges improperly. The previous question is often abused and used tyrannically; but on the whole it is a most invaluable aid to legislation. Benton, however, waxed hot and wrathful over the proposed change in the Senate rules. He, with Calhoun and their followers, had been consuming an immense amount of time in speech-making against the Whig measures, and in offering amendments; not with any hopes of bettering the bills, but for outside effect, and to annoy their opponents. He gives an amusingly naive account of their course of action, and the reasons for it, substantially as follows:—

> The Democratic senators acted upon a system, and with a thorough organization and a perfect understanding. Being a minority, and able to do nothing, they became assailants, and attacked incessantly; not by formal orations against the whole body of a measure, but by sudden, short, and

pungent speeches directed against the vulnerable parts, and pointed by proffered amendments. Amendments were continually offered—a great number being prepared every night and placed in suitable hands for use the next day—always commendably calculated to expose an evil and to present a remedy. Near forty propositions of amendment were offered to the first fiscal agent bill alone—the yeas and nays were taken upon them seven and thirty times. All the other prominent bills—distribution, bankrupt, fiscal corporation, new tariff act, called revenue—were served the same way; every proposed amendment made an issue. There were but twenty-two of us, but every one was a speaker and effective. The "Globe" newspaper was a powerful ally, setting out all we did to the best advantage in strong editorials, and carrying out our speeches, fresh and hot, to the people; and we felt victorious in the midst of unbroken defeats.

It is no wonder that such rank filibustering, coupled with the exasperating self-complacency of its originators, should have excited in Whig bosoms every desperate emotion short of homicidal mania.

Clay, to cut off such useless talk, gave notice that he would move to have the time for debate for each individual restricted; remarking very truthfully that he did not believe the people at large would complain of the abridgment of speeches in Congress. But the Democratic senators, all rather fond of windy orations, fairly foamed at the mouth at what they affected to deem such an infringement of their liberties; and actually took the inexcusable resolution of bidding defiance to the rule if it was adopted, and refusing to obey it, no matter what degree of violence their conduct might bring about,—a resolution that was wholly unpardonable. Benton was selected to voice their views upon the matter, which he did in a long, and not very wise speech; while Calhoun was quite as emphatic in his threats of what would happen if attempt should be made to enforce the proposed rule. Clay was always much bolder in opening a campaign than in carrying it through; and when it came to putting his words into deeds, he wholly lacked the nerve which would have enabled him to contend with two such men as the senators from Missouri and South Carolina. Had he possessed a temperament like that of either of his opponents, he would have gone on and have simply forced acquiescence; for any legislative body can certainly enforce what rules it may choose to make as to the conduct of its own members in addressing it; but his courage failed him, and he withdrew from the contest, leaving the victory with Democrats.

When the question of the re-charter of the district banks came up, it of course gave Benton another chance to attack his favorite foe. He offered a very proper amendment, which was voted down, to prohibit the banks from issuing a currency of small notes, fixing upon twenty dollars as being the lowest limit. This he supported in a strong speech, wherein he once again argued at length in favor of a gold and silver currency, and showed the evil effects of small bank-notes, which might not be, and often were not, redeemable at par. He very properly pointed out that to have a sound currency, especially in all the smaller denominations, was really of greater interest to the working men than to any one else.

The great measure of the session, however, and the one that was intended to be the final crown and glory of the Whig triumph, was the bill to establish a new national bank. Among the political theories to which Clay clung most closely, only the belief in a bank ranked higher in his estimation than his devotion to a protective tariff. The establishment of a national bank seemed to him to be the chief object of a Whig success; and that it would work immediate and immense benefit to the country was with him an article of faith. With both houses of Congress under his control, he at once prepared to push his pet measure through, impatiently brushing aside all resistance.

But at the very outset difficulty was feared from the action of the president. Tyler could not at first make up his mind what to do; or rather, he made it up in half a dozen different ways every day. His peevishness, vacillation, ambitious vanity, and sheer puzzle-headedness made him incline first to the side of his new friends and present supporters, the Whigs, and then to that of his old democratic allies, whose views on the bank, as on most other questions, he had so often openly expressed himself as sharing. But though his mind oscillated like a pendulum, yet each time it swung farther and farther over to the side of the Democracy, and it began to look as if he would certainly in the end come to a halt in the camp of the enemies of the Whigs; his approach to this destination was merely hastened by Clay's overbearing violence and injudicious taunts.

However, at first Tyler did not dare to come out openly against any and all bank laws, but tried to search round for some compromise measure; and as he could not invent a compromise in fact, he came to the conclusion that one in words would do just as well. He said that his conscience would not permit him to sign a bill to establish a bank that was called a bank, but that he was willing to sign a bill establishing such an institution provided that it was called something else, though it should possess all the properties of a bank. Such a proposal opened a wide field for the endless quibbling in which his soul delighted.

The secretary of the treasury, in response to a call from the Senate, furnished a plan for a bank, having modeled it studiously so as to overcome the president's scruples; and a select committee of the Senate at once shaped a bill in accordance with the plans. Said Benton: "Even the title was made ridiculous to please the president, though not so much so as he wished. He objected to the name of bank either in the title or the body of the charter, and proposed to style it 'Fiscal Institute;' and afterwards the 'Fiscal Agent,' and finally the 'Fiscal Corporation.'" Such preposterous folly on the president's part was more than the hot-blooded and overbearing Kentuckian could stand; and, in spite of his absorbing desire for the success of his measure, and of the vital necessity for conciliating Tyler, Clay could not bring himself to adopt such a ludicrous title, even though he had seen that the charter provided that the institution, whatever it might be styled in form, should in fact have all the properties of a bank. After a while, however, a compromise title was agreed on, but only a shadow less imbecile than the original one proposed by the president; and it was agreed to call the measure the "Fiscal Bank" bill.

The president vetoed it, but stated that he was ready to approve any similar bill that should be free from the objections he named. Clay could not resist reading Tyler a lecture on his misconduct, during the course of a speech in the Senate; but the Whigs generally smothered their resentment, and set about preparing something which the president would sign, and this time concluded that they would humor him to the top of his bent, even by choosing a title as ridiculous as he wished; so they styled their bill one to establish a "Fiscal Corporation." Benton held the title up to well-deserved derision, and showed that, though there had been quite an elaborate effort to disguise the form of the measure, and to make it purport to establish a bank that should have the properties of a treasury, yet that in reality it was simply a revival of the old scheme under another name. The Whigs swallowed the sneers of their opponents as best they could, and passed their bill.

The president again interposed his veto. An intrigue was going on among a few unimportant congressmen and obscure office-holders to form a new party with Tyler at its head; and the latter willingly entered into the plan, his mind, which was not robust at the best, being completely dazzled by his sudden elevation and his wild hopes that he could continue to keep the place which he had reached. He had given the Whigs reason to expect that he would sign the bill, and had taken none of his cabinet into his confidence. So, when his veto came in, it raised a perfect whirlwind of wrath and bitter disappointment. His cabinet all resigned, except Webster, who stayed to finish the treaty with Great Britain; and the Whigs formally read him out of the party. The Democrats looked on with huge enjoyment, and patted Tyler on the back, for they could see that he was bringing their foes to ruin; but nevertheless they despised him heartily, and abandoned him wholly when he had served their turn. Left without any support among the regulars of either side, and his own proposed third party turning out a still-born abortion, he simply played out his puny part until his term ended, and then dropped noiselessly out of sight. It is only the position he filled, and not in the least his ability, for either good or bad, in filling it, that prevents his name from sinking into merciful oblivion.

There was yet one more brief spasm over the bank, however; the president sending in a plan for a "Fiscal Agent," to be called a Board of Exchequer. Congress contemptuously refused to pay any attention to the proposition, Benton showing its utter unworthiness in an excellent speech, one of the best that he made on the whole financial question.

Largely owing to the cross purposes at which the president and his party were working, the condition of the treasury became very bad. It sought to provide for its immediate wants by the issue of treasury notes, differing from former notes of the kind in that they were made reissuable. Benton at once, and very properly, attacked this proceeding. He had a check drawn for a few days' compensation as senator, demanded payment in hard money, and when he was given treasury notes instead, made a most emphatic protest in the Senate, which was entirely effectual, the practically compulsory tender of the paper money being forthwith stopped.

It was at this time, also, that bills to subsidize steamship lines were first passed, and that the enlarging and abuse of the pension system began, which in our own day threatens to become a really crying evil. Benton opposed both sets of measures; and in regard to the pension matter showed that he would not let himself, by any specious plea of exceptional suffering or need for charity, be led into vicious special legislation, sure in the end to bring about the breaking down of some of the most important principles of government.

CHAPTER XII.

BOUNDARY TROUBLES WITH ENGLAND.

Two important controversies with foreign powers became prominent during Tyler's presidency; but he had little to do with the settlement of either, beyond successively placing in his cabinet the two great statesmen who dealt with them. Webster, while secretary of state, brought certain of the negotiations with England to a close; and later on, Calhoun, while holding the same office, took up Webster's work and also grappled with—indeed partly caused—the troubles on the Mexican border, and turned them to the advantage of the South and slavery.

Our boundaries were still very ill-defined, except where they were formed by the Gulf and the Ocean, the Great Lakes, and the river St. John. Even in the Northeast, where huge stretches of unbroken forest-land separated the inhabited portions of Canada from those of New England, it was not yet decided how much of this wilderness belonged to us and how much to the Canadians; and in the vast, unsettled regions of the far West our claims came into direct conflict with those of Mexico and of Great Britain. The ownership of these little known and badly mapped regions could with great difficulty be decided on grounds of absolute and abstract right; the title of each contestant to the land was more or less plausible, and at the same time more or less defective. The matter was sure to be decided in favor of the strongest; and, say what we will about the justice and right of the various claims, the honest truth is, that the comparative might of the different nations, and not the comparative righteousness of their several causes, was the determining factor in the settlement. Mexico lost her northern provinces by no law of right, but simply by the law of the longest sword—the same law that gave India to England. In both instances the result was greatly to the benefit of the conquered peoples and of every one else; though there is this wide difference between the two cases: that whereas the English rule in India, while it may last for decades or even for centuries, must eventually come to an end and leave little trace of its existence; on the other hand our conquests from Mexico determined for all time the blood, speech, and law of the men who should fill the lands we won.

The questions between Great Britain and ourselves were compromised by each side accepting about half what it claimed, only because neither was willing to push the other to extremities. Englishmen like Palmerston might hector and ruffle, and Americans like Benton might swagger and bully; but when it came to be a question of actual fighting each people recognized the power of the other, and preferred to follow the more cautious and peaceful, not to say timid, lead of such statesmen as Webster and Lord Melbourne.

Had we been no stronger than the Sikhs, Oregon and Washington would at present be British possessions; and if Great Britain had been as weak as Mexico, she would not now hold a foot of territory on the Pacific coast. Either nation might perhaps have refused to commit a gross and entirely unprovoked and uncalled-for act of aggression; but each, under altered conditions, would have readily found excuses for showing much less regard for the claims of the other than actually was shown. It would be untrue to say that nations have not at times proved themselves capable of acting with great disinterestedness and generosity towards other peoples; but such conduct is not very common at the best, and although it often may be desirable, it certainly is not always so. If the matter in dispute is of great importance, and if there is a doubt as to which side is right, then the strongest party to the controversy is pretty sure to give itself the benefit of that doubt; and international morality will have to take tremendous strides in advance before this ceases to be the case.

It is difficult to exaggerate the importance of the treaties and wars by means of which we finally gave definite bounds to our territory beyond the Mississippi. Contemporary political writers and students, of the lesser sort, are always painfully deficient in the sense of historic perspective; and to such the struggles for the possession of the unknown and dimly outlined western wastes seemed of small consequence compared to similar European contests for territorial aggrandizement. Yet, in reality, when we look at the far-reaching nature of the results, the questions as to what kingdom should receive the fealty of Holstein or Lorraine, of Savoy or the Dobrudscha, seem of absolutely trivial importance compared to the infinitely more momentous ones as to the future race settlement and national ownership of the then lonely and unpeopled lands of Texas, California, and Oregon.

Benton, greatly to the credit of his foresight, and largely in consequence of his strong nationalist feeling, thoroughly appreciated the importance of our geographical extensions. He was the great champion of the West and of western development, and a furious partisan of every movement in the direction of the enlargement of our western boundaries. Many of his expressions, when talking of the greatness of our country and of the magnitude of the interests which were being decided, not only were grandiloquent in manner, but also seem exaggerated and overwrought even as regards matter. But when we think of the interests for which he contended, as they were to become, and not as they at the moment were, the appearance of exaggeration is lost, and the intense feeling of his speeches no longer seems out of place or disproportionate to the importance of the subject with which he dealt. Without clearly formulating his opinions, even to himself, and while sometimes prone to attribute to his country at the moment a greatness she was not to possess for two or three generations to come, he, nevertheless, had engrained in his very marrow and fibre the knowledge that inevitably, and beyond all doubt, the coming years were to be hers. He knew that, while other nations held the past, and shared with his own the present, yet that to her belonged the still formless and unshaped future. More clearly than almost any other statesman he beheld the grandeur of the nation loom up, vast and shadowy, through the advancing years.

He was keenly alive to the need of our having free chance to spread towards the northwest; he very early grasped the idea that in that direction we ought to have room for continental development. In his earliest years, to be sure, when the Mississippi seemed a river of the remote western border, when nobody, not even the hardiest trapper, had penetrated the boundless and treeless plains that stretch to the foot-hills of the Rockies, and when the boldest thinkers had not dared to suppose that we could ever hold together as a people, when once scattered over so wide a territory, he had stated in a public speech that he considered the mountains to be our natural frontier line to the west, and the barrier beyond which we ought not to pass, and had expressed his trust that on the Pacific coast there would grow up a kindred and friendly Republic. But very soon, as the seemingly impossible became the actual, he himself changed, and ever afterwards held that we should have, wherever possible, no boundaries but the two Oceans.

Benton's violent and aggressive patriotism undoubtedly led him to assume positions towards foreign powers that were very repugnant to the quiet, peaceable, and order-loving portion of the community, especially when he gave vent to the spirit of jealous antagonism which he felt towards Great Britain, the power that held sway over the wilderness bordering us on the north. Yet the arrogant attitude he assumed was more than justified by the destiny of the great Republic; and it would have been well for all America if we had insisted even more than we did upon the extension northward of our boundaries. Not only the Columbia but also the Red River of the North— and the Saskatchewan and Frazer as well—should lie wholly within our limits, less for our own sake than for the sake of the men who dwell along their banks. Columbia, Saskatchewan, and Manitoba would, as states of the American Union, hold positions incomparably more important, grander, and more dignified than they can ever hope to reach either as independent communities or as provincial dependencies of a foreign power that regards them with a kindly tolerance somewhat akin to contemptuous indifference. Of course no one would wish to see these, or any other settled communities, now added to our domain by force; we want no unwilling citizens to enter our Union; the time to have taken the lands was before settlers came into them. European nations war for the possession of thickly settled districts which, if conquered, will for centuries remain alien and hostile to the conquerors; we, wiser in our generation, have seized the waste solitudes that lay near us, the limitless forests and never ending plains, and the valleys of the great, lonely rivers; and have thrust our own sons into them to take possession; and a score of years after each conquest we see the conquered land teeming with a people that is one with ourselves.

Benton felt that all the unoccupied land to the northwest was by right our heritage, and he was willing to do battle for it if necessary. He was a perfect type of western American statesmanship in his way of looking at our foreign relations; he was always unwilling to compromise, being of that happy temperament which is absolutely certain that its claims are just and righteous in their entirety, and that it would be wrong to accept anything less than all that is demanded; he was willing to bully if our rights, as he deemed them, were not granted us; and he was perfectly ready to fight if the bullying was unsuccessful. True, he did not consistently carry through all his theories to their logical consequences; but it may well be questioned whether, after all, his original attitude towards Great Britain was not wiser, looking to its probable remote results, than that which was finally taken by the national government, whose policy was on this point largely shaped by the feeling among the richer and more educated classes of the Northeast. These classes have always been more cautious and timid than any others in the Union, especially in their way of looking at possible foreign wars, and have never felt much of the spirit which made the West stretch out impatiently for new lands. Fortunately they have rarely been able to control our territorial growth.

No foot of soil to which we had any title in the Northwest should have been given up; we were the people who could use it best, and we ought to have taken it all. The prize was well worth winning, and would warrant a good deal of risk being run. We had even then grown to be so strong that we were almost sure eventually to win in any American contest for continental supremacy. We were near by, our foes far away—for the contest over the Columbia would have been settled in Canada. We should have had hard fighting to be sure, but sooner or later the result would have been in our favor. There were no better soldiers in the world than the men of Balaclava and Inkerman, but the victors of Buena Vista and Chapultepec were as good. Scott and Taylor were not great generals, but they were, at least, the equals of Lord Raglan; and we did not have in our service any such examples of abnormal military inaptitude as Lords Lucan and Cardigan and their kind.

It was of course to be expected that men like Benton would bitterly oppose the famous Ashburton treaty, which was Webster's crowning work while secretary of state, and the only conspicuous success of Tyler's administration. The Ashburton treaty was essentially a compromise between the extreme claims of the two contestants, as was natural where the claims were based on very unsubstantial grounds and the contestants were of somewhat the same strength. It was most beneficial in its immediate effects; and that it was a perfectly dignified and proper treaty for America to make is best proved by the virulent hostility with which Palmerston and his followers assailed it as a "surrender" on the part of England, while Englishmen of the same stamp are to this day never tired of lamenting the fact that they have allowed our western boundaries to be pushed so far to the north. But there appears to be much excuse for Benton's attitude, when we look at the treaty as one in a chain of incidents, and with regard to its future results. Our territorial quarrels with Great Britain were not like those between most other powers. It was for the interest of the whole western hemisphere that no European nation should have extensive possessions between the Atlantic and the Pacific; and by right we should have given ourselves the benefit of every doubt in all territorial questions, and have shown ourselves ready to make prompt appeal to the sword whenever it became necessary as a last resort.

Still, as regards the Ashburton treaty itself, it must be admitted that much of Benton's opposition was merely factious and partisan, on account of its being a Whig measure; and his speeches on the subject contain a number of arguments that are not very creditable to him.

Some of his remarks referred to a matter which had been already a cause of great excitement during Van Buren's administration, and on which he had spoken more than once. This was the destruction of the steamer Caroline by the British during the abortive Canadian insurrection of 1837. Much sympathy had been felt for the rebels by the Americans along the border, and some of them had employed the Caroline in conveying stores to the insurgents; and in revenge a party of British troops surprised and destroyed her one night while she was lying in an American port. This was a gross and flagrant violation of our rights, and was promptly resented by Van Buren, who had done what he could to maintain order along the border, and had been successful in his efforts. Benton had supported the president in preventing a breach of neutrality on our part, and was fiercely indignant when the breach was committed by the other side. Reparation was demanded forthwith. The British government at first made evasive replies. After a while a very foolish personage named McLeod, a British subject, who boasted that he had taken part in the affair, ventured into New York and was promptly imprisoned by the state authorities. His boastings, fortunately for him, proved to be totally unfounded, and he was acquitted by the jury before whom he was taken, after a detention of several months in prison. But meanwhile the British government demanded his release—adopting a very different tone with Tyler and the Whigs from that which they had been using towards Van Buren, who still could conjure with Jackson's terrible name. The United States agreed to release McLeod, but New York refused to deliver him up; and before the question was decided he was acquitted, as said above. It was clearly wrong for a state to interfere in a disagreement between the nation and a foreign power; and on the other hand the federal authorities did not show as much firmness in their dealings with England as they should have shown. Benton, true to certain of his states-rights theories and in pursuance of his policy of antagonism to Great Britain, warmly supported the attitude of New York, alleging that the United States had no right to interfere with her disposal of McLeod; and asserting that while if the citizens of one country committed an outrage upon another it was necessary to apply to the sovereign for redress, yet that if the wrong-doers came into the country which had been aggrieved they might be seized and punished; and he exultingly referred to Jackson's conduct at the time of the first Seminole War, when he hung off-hand two British subjects whom he accused of inciting the Indians against us, Great Britain not making any protest. The Caroline matter was finally settled in the Ashburton treaty, the British making a formal but very guarded apology for her destruction,—an apology which did not satisfy Benton in the least.

It is little to Benton's credit, however, that, while thus courting foreign wars, he yet opposed the efforts of the Whigs to give us a better navy. Our navy was then good of its kind, but altogether too small. Benton's opposition to its increase seems to have proceeded partly from mere bitter partisanship, partly from sheer ignorance, and partly from the doctrinaire dread of any kind of standing military or naval force, which he had inherited, with a good many similar ideas, from the Jeffersonians.

He attacked the whole treaty, article by article, when it came up for ratification in the Senate, making an extremely lengthy and elaborate speech, or rather set of speeches, against it. Much of his objection, especially to the part compromising the territorial claims of the two governments, was well founded; but much was also factious and groundless. The most important point of all that was in controversy, the ownership of Oregon, was left unsettled; but, as will be shown farther on, this was wise. He made this omission a base or pretext for the charge that the treaty was gotten up in the interests of the East,—although with frank lack of logic he also opposed it because it sacrificed the interests of Maine,—and that it was detrimental to the South and West; and he did his best to excite sectional feeling against it. He also protested against the omission of all reference to the impressment of American sailors by British vessels; and this was a valid ground of opposition,—although Webster had really settled the matter by writing a formal note to the British government, in which he practically gave official notice that any attempt to revive the practice would be repelled by force of arms.

Benton occupied a much less tenable position when he came to the question of slavery, and inveighed against the treaty because it did not provide for the return of fugitive slaves, or of slaves taken from American coasting vessels when the latter happened to be obliged to put into West Indian ports, and because it did contain a provision that we ourselves should keep in commission a squadron on the coast of Africa to coöperate with the British in the suppression of the slave-trade. Benton's object in attacking the treaty on this point was to excite the South to a degree that would make the senators from that section refuse to join in ratifying it; but the attempt was a flat failure. It is hardly to be supposed that he himself was as indignant over this question as he pretended to be. He must have realized that, so long as we had among ourselves an institution so wholly barbarous and out of date as slavery, just so long we should have to expect foreign powers to treat us rather cavalierly on that one point. Whatever we might say among ourselves as to the rights of property or the necessity of preserving the Union by refraining from the disturbance of slavery, it was certain that foreign nations would place the manhood and liberty of the slave above the vested interest of the master—all the more readily because they were jealous of the Union and anxious to see it break up, and were naturally delighted to take the side of abstract justice and humanity, when to do so was at the expense of outsiders and redounded to their own credit, without causing them the least pecuniary loss or personal inconvenience. The attitude of slave-holders towards freedom in the abstract was grotesque in its lack of logic; but the attitude of many other classes of men, both abroad and at home, towards it was equally full of a grimly unconscious humor. The southern planters, who loudly sympathized with Kossuth and the Hungarians, were entirely unconscious that their tyranny over their own black bondsmen made their attacks upon Austria's despotism absurd; and Germans, who were shocked at our holding the blacks in slavery, could not think of freedom in their own country without a shudder. On one night the Democrats of the Northern States would hold a mass meeting to further the cause of Irish freedom, on the next night the same men would break up another meeting held to help along the freeing of the negroes; while the English aristocracy held up its hands in horror at American slavery and set its face like a flint against all efforts to do Ireland tardy and incomplete justice.

Again, in his opposition to the extradition clause of the treaty, Benton was certainly wrong. Nothing is clearer than that nations ought to combine to prevent criminals from escaping punishment merely by fleeing over an imaginary line; the crime is against all society, and society should unite to punish it. Especially is there need of the most stringent extradition laws between countries whose people have the same speech and legal system, as with the United States and Great Britain. Indeed, it is a pity that our extradition laws are not more stringent. But Benton saw, or affected to see, in the extradition clause, a menace to political refugees, and based his opposition to it mainly on this ground. He also quoted on his side the inevitable Jefferson; for Jefferson, or rather the highly idealized conception of what Jefferson had been, shared with the "demos krateo principle" the honor of being one of the twin fetiches to which Benton, in common with most of his fellow-Democrats, especially delighted to bow down.

But when he came to the parts of the treaty that defined our northeastern boundary and so much of our northwestern boundary as lay near the Great Lakes, Benton occupied far more defensible ground; and the parts of his speech referring to these questions were very strong indeed. He attempted to show that in the matter of the Maine frontier we had surrendered very much more than there was any need of our doing, and that the British claim was unfounded; and there seems now to be good reason for thinking him right, although it must be admitted that in agreeing to the original line in earlier treaties the British had acted entirely under a misapprehension as to where it would go. Benton was also able to make a good point against Webster for finally agreeing to surrender so much of Maine's claim by showing the opposition the latter had made, while in the Senate, to a similar but less objectionable clause in a treaty which Jackson's administration had then been trying to get through. Again Webster had, in defending the surrender of certain of our claims along the boundary west of Lake Superior, stated that the country was not very valuable, as it was useless for agricultural purposes; and Benton had taken him up sharply on this point, saying that we wanted the land anyhow, whether it produced corn and potatoes or only furs and lumber. The amounts of territory as to which our claims were compromised were not very large compared to the extent of the Pacific coast lands which were still left in dispute; and it was perhaps well that the treaty was ratified; but certainly there is much to be said on Benton's side so far as his opposition to the proposed frontier was concerned.

However, he was only able to rally eight other senators to his support, and the treaty went through the Senate triumphantly. It encountered an even more bitter opposition in Parliament, where Palmerston headed a series of furious attacks upon it, for reasons the precise opposite of those which Benton alleged, arguing that England received much less, instead of much more, than her due, and thereby showing Webster's position in a very much better light than that in which it would otherwise have appeared. Eventually the British government ratified the treaty.

The Ashburton treaty did not touch on the Oregon matter at all; nor was this dealt with by Webster while he was secretary of state. But it came before the Senate at that time, and later on Calhoun took it up, when filling Webster's place in the cabinet, although a final decision was not reached until during Polk's presidency. Webster did not appreciate the importance of Oregon in the least, and moreover came from a section of the country that was not inclined to insist on territorial expansion at the hazard of a war, in which the merchants of the sea-board would be the chief sufferers. Calhoun, it is true, came from a peculiarly militant and bellicose state, but on the other hand from a section that was not very anxious to see the free North acquire new territory. So it happened that neither of Tyler's two great secretaries felt called upon to insist too vehemently upon going to extremes in defense of our rights, or supposed rights, along the Pacific coast; and though in the end the balance was struck pretty evenly between our claims and those of our neighbor, yet it is to be regretted that we did not stand out stiffly for the whole of our demand. Our title was certainly not perfect, but it was to the full as good as, or better than, Great Britain's; and it would have been better in the end had we insisted upon the whole territory being given to us, no matter what price we had to pay.

The politico-social line of division between the East and the West had been gradually growing fainter as that between the North and South grew deeper; but on the Oregon question it again became prominent. Southeastern Democrats, like the Carolinian McDuffie, spoke as slightingly of the value of Oregon, and were as little inclined to risk a war for its possession, as the most peace-loving Whigs of New England; while the intense western feeling against giving up any of our rights on the Pacific coast was best expressed by the two senators from the slave state of Missouri. Benton was not restrained in his desire to add to the might of the Union by any fear of the possible future effect upon the political power of the Slave States. Although a slave-holder and the representative of slave-holders, he was fully alive to the evils of slavery, though as yet not seeing clearly how all-important a question it had become. The preservation and extension of the Union and obedience to the spirit of Democracy were the chief articles of his political creed, and to these he always subordinated all others. When, in speaking of slavery, he made use, as he sometimes did, of expressions that were not far removed from those of men really devoted to the slave interests, it was almost always because he had some ulterior object in view, or for factional ends; for unfortunately his standard of political propriety was not sufficiently high to prevent his trying to make use of any weapon, good or bad, with which to overturn his political foes. In protesting against the Ashburton treaty, he outdid even such slavery champions as Calhoun in the extravagance of his ideas as to what we should demand of foreign powers in reference to their treatment of our "peculiar institution"; but he seems to have done this merely because thereby he got an additional handle of attack against the Whig measures. The same thing was true earlier of his fulmination against Clay's proposed Panama Congress; and even before that, in attacking Adams for his supposed part in the treaty whereby we established the line of our Spanish frontier, he dragged slavery into the question, not, apparently, because he really particularly wished to see our slave territory extended, but because he thought that he might use the slavery cry to excite in one other section of the country a feeling as strong as that which the West already felt in regard to territorial expansion generally. Indeed, his whole conduct throughout the Oregon controversy, especially when taken in connection with the fact that he stood out for Maine's frontier rights more stoutly than the Maine representatives themselves, shows how free from sectional bias was his way of looking at our geographical growth.

The territory along the Pacific coast lying between California on the south and Alaska on the north—"Oregon," as it was comprehensively called—had been a source of dispute for some time between the United States and Great Britain. After some negotiations both had agreed with Russia to recognize the line of 54° 40' as the southern boundary of the latter's possessions; and Mexico's undisputed possession of California gave an equally well marked southern limit, at the forty-second parallel. All between was in dispute. The British had trading posts at the mouth of the Columbia, which they emphatically asserted to be theirs; we, on the other hand, claimed an absolutely clear title up to the forty-ninth parallel, a couple of hundred miles north of the mouth of the Columbia, and asserted that for all the balance of the territory up to the Russian possessions our title was at any rate better than that of the British. In 1818 a treaty had been made providing for the joint occupation of the territory by the two powers, as neither was willing to give up its claim to the whole, or at the time at all understood the value of the possession, then entirely unpeopled. This treaty of joint occupancy had remained in force ever since. Under it the British had built great trading stations, and used the whole country in the interests of certain fur companies. The Americans, in spite of some vain efforts, were unable to compete with them in this line; but, what was infinitely more important, had begun, even prior to 1840, to establish actual settlers along the banks of the rivers, some missionaries being the first to come in. As long, however, as the territory remained sparsely settled, and the communication with it chiefly by sea, the hold of Great Britain gave promise of being the stronger. But the aspect of affairs was totally changed when in 1842 a huge caravan of over a thousand Americans made the journey overland from the frontiers of Missouri, taking with them their wives and their children, their flocks and herds, carrying their long rifles on their shoulders, and their axes and spades in the great canvas-topped wagons. The next year, two thousand more settlers of the same sort in their turn crossed the vast plains, wound their way among the Rocky Mountains through the pass explored by Fremont, Benton's son-in-law, and after suffering every kind of hardship and danger, and warding off the attacks of hostile Indians, descended the western slope of the great water-shed to join their fellows by the banks of the Columbia. When American settlers were once in actual possession of the disputed territory, it became evident that the period of Great Britain's undisputed sway was over.

The government of the United States, meanwhile, was so far from helping these settlers that it on the contrary rather threw obstacles in their way. As usual with us, the individual activity of the citizens themselves, who all acted independently and with that peculiar self-reliance that is the chief American characteristic, outstripped the activity of their representatives, who were obliged all to act together, and who were therefore held back by each other,—our Constitution, while giving free scope for individual freedom, wisely providing such checks as to make our governmental system eminently conservative in its workings. Tyler's administration did not wish to embroil itself with England; so it refused any aid to the settlers, and declined to give them grants of land, as under the joint occupancy treaty that would have given England offense and cause for complaint. But Benton and the other Westerners were perfectly willing to offend England, if by so doing they could help America to obtain Oregon, and were too rash and headstrong to count the cost of their actions. Accordingly, a bill was introduced providing for the settlement of Oregon, and giving each settler six hundred and forty acres, and additional land if he had a family; so that every inducement was held out to the emigrants, the West wanting to protect and encourage them by all the means in its power. The laws and jurisdiction of the Territory of Iowa were to be extended to all the settlers on the Pacific coast, who hitherto had governed themselves merely by a system of mutual agreements.

The bill was, of course, strongly opposed, especially on account of the clause giving land to the settlers. It passed the Senate by a close vote, but failed in the House. Naturally Benton was one of its chief supporters, and spoke at length in its favor. He seized the kernel of the matter when, in advocating the granting of land, he spoke of immigration as "the only thing which can save the country from the British, acting through their powerful agent, the Hudson's Bay Company." He then blew a lusty note of defiance to Great Britain herself:—

> I think she will take offense, do what we may in relation to this territory. She wants it herself, and means to quarrel for it, if she does not fight for it.... I grant that she will take offense, but that is not the question with me. Has she a *right* to take offense? That is my question! And this being decided in the negative, I neither fear nor calculate consequences.... Courage will keep her off, fear will bring her upon us. The assertion of our rights will command her respect; the fear to assert them will bring us her contempt.... Neither nations nor individuals ever escaped danger by fearing it. They must face it and defy it. An abandonment of a right for fear of bringing on an attack, instead of keeping it off, will inevitably bring on the outrage that is dreaded.

He was right enough in his disposition to resent the hectoring spirit which, at that time, characterized Great Britain's foreign policy; but he was all wrong in condemning delay, and stating that if things were left as they were time would work against us, and not for us.

In this respect Calhoun, who opposed the bill, was much wiser. He advocated a policy of "masterly inactivity," foreseeing that time was everything to us, inasmuch as the land was sure in the end to belong to that nation whose people had settled in it, and we alone were able to furnish a constantly increasing stream of immigrants. Later on, however, Calhoun abandoned this policy, probably mainly influenced by fear of the extension of free territory, and consented to a compromise with Great Britain. The true course to have pursued would have been to have combined the ideas of both Benton and Calhoun, and to have gone farther than either; that is, we should have allowed the question to remain unsettled as long as was possible, because every year saw an increasing American population in the coveted lands, and rendered the ultimate decision surer to be for us. When it was impossible to postpone the question longer, we should have insisted upon its being settled entirely in our favor, no matter at what cost. The unsuccessful attempts, made by Benton and his supporters, to persuade the Senate to pass a resolution, requiring that notice of the termination of the joint occupancy treaty should forthwith be given, were certainly ill-advised.

However, even Benton was not willing to go to the length to which certain Western men went, who insisted upon all or nothing. He had become alarmed and angry over the intrigue for the admission of Texas and the proposed forcible taking away of Mexican territory. The Northwestern Democrats wanted all Texas and all Oregon; the Southeastern ones wished all the former and part of the latter. Benton then concluded that it would be best to take part of each; for, although no friend to compromises, yet he was unwilling to jeopardize the safety of the Union as it was by seeking to make it still larger. Accordingly, he sympathized with the effort made by Calhoun while secretary of state to get the British to accept the line of 49° as the frontier; but the British government then rejected this proposition. In 1844 the Democrats made their campaign upon the issue of "fifty-four forty or fight;" and Polk, when elected, felt obliged to insist upon this campaign boundary. To this, however, Great Britain naturally would not consent; it was, indeed, idle to expect her to do so, unless things should be kept as they were until a fairly large American population had grown up along the Pacific coast, and had thus put her in a position where she could hardly do anything else. Polk's administration was neither capable nor warlike, however well disposed to bluster; and the secretary of state, the timid, shifty, and selfish politician, Buchanan, naturally fond of facing both ways, was the last man to wish to force a quarrel on a high-spirited and determined antagonist like

England. Accordingly, he made up his mind to back down and try for the line of 49°, as proposed by Calhoun, when in Tyler's cabinet; and the English, for all their affected indifference, had been so much impressed by the warlike demonstrations in the United States, that they in turn were delighted, singing in a much lower key than before the "fifty-four forty" cry had been raised; accordingly they withdrew their former pretensions to the Columbia River and accepted the offered compromise. Now, however, came the question of getting the treaty through the Senate; and Buchanan sounded Benton, to see if he would undertake this task.

Benton, worried over the Texas matter, was willing to recede somewhat from the very high ground he had taken,—although, of course, he insisted that he had been perfectly consistent throughout, and that the 49th parallel was the line he had all along been striving for. Under his lead the proposal for a treaty on the basis indicated was carried through the Senate, and the line in consequence ultimately became our frontier, in spite of the frantic opposition of the Northwestern Democrats, the latter hurling every sort of charge of bad faith and treachery at their Southern associates, who had joined with the Whigs in defeating them. Benton's speech in support of the proposal was pitched much lower than had been his previous ones; and, a little forgetful of some of his own remarks, he was especially severe upon those members who denounced England and held up a picture of her real or supposed designs to excite and frighten the people into needless opposition to her.

In its immediate effects the adoption of the 49th parallel as the dividing line between the two countries was excellent, and entailed no loss of dignity on either. Yet, as there was no particular reason why we should show any generosity in our diplomatic dealings with England, it may well be questioned whether it would not have been better to have left things as they were until we could have taken all. Wars are, of course, as a rule to be avoided; but they are far better than certain kinds of peace. Every war in which we have been engaged, except the one with Mexico, has been justifiable in its origin; and each one, without any exception whatever, has left us better off, taking both moral and material considerations into account, than we should have been if we had not waged it.

CHAPTER XIII.

THE ABOLITIONISTS DANCE TO THE SLAVE BARONS' PIPING.

In 1844 the Whig candidate for the Presidency, Henry Clay, was defeated by a Mr. Polk, the nominee of the Democracy. The majorities in several of the states were very small; this was the case, for example in New York, the change in whose electoral vote would have also changed the entire result.

Up to 1860 there were very few political contests in which the dividing lines between right and wrong so nearly coincided with those drawn between the two opposing parties as in that of 1844. The Democrats favored the annexation of Texas, and the addition of new slave territory to the Union; the Whigs did not. Almost every good element in the country stood behind Clay; the vast majority of intelligent, high-minded, upright men supported him. Polk was backed by rabid Southern fire-eaters and slavery extensionists, who had deified negro bondage and exalted it beyond the Union, the Constitution, and everything else; by the almost solid foreign vote, still unfit for the duties of American citizenship; by the vicious and criminal classes in all the great cities of the North and in New Orleans; by the corrupt politicians, who found ignorance and viciousness tools ready forged to their hands, wherewith to perpetrate the gigantic frauds without which the election would have been lost; and, lastly, he was also backed indirectly but most powerfully by the political Abolitionists.

These Abolitionists had formed themselves into the Liberty party, and ran Birney for president; and though they polled but little over sixty thousand votes, yet as these were drawn almost entirely from the ranks of Clay's supporters, they were primarily responsible for his defeat; for the defections were sufficiently large to turn the scale in certain pivotal and closely contested states, notably New York. Their action in this case was wholly evil, alike in its immediate and its remote results; they simply played into the hands of the extreme slavery men like Calhoun, and became, for the time being, the willing accomplices of the latter. Yet they would have accomplished nothing had it not been for the frauds and outrages perpetrated by the gangs of native and foreign-born ruffians in the great cities, under the leadership of such brutal rowdies as Isaiah Rynders.

These three men, Calhoun, Birney, and Isaiah Rynders, may be taken as types of the classes that were chiefly instrumental in the election of Polk, and that must, therefore, bear the responsibility for all the evils attendant thereon, including among them the bloody and unrighteous war with Mexico. With the purpose of advancing the cause of abstract right, but with the result of sacrificing all that was best, most honest, and most high-principled in national politics, the Abolitionists joined hands with Northern roughs and Southern slavocrats to elect the man who was, excepting Tyler, the very smallest of the line of small presidents who came in between Jackson and Lincoln.

Owing to a variety of causes, the Abolitionists have received an immense amount of hysterical praise, which they do not deserve, and have been credited with deeds done by other men, whom they in reality hampered and opposed rather than aided. After 1840 the professed Abolitionists formed but a small and comparatively unimportant portion of the forces that were working towards the restriction and ultimate destruction of slavery; and much of what they did was positively harmful to the cause for which they were fighting. Those of their number who considered the Constitution as a league with death and hell, and who therefore advocated a dissolution of the Union, acted as rationally as would anti-polygamists nowadays if, to show their disapproval of Mormonism, they should advocate that Utah should be allowed to form a separate nation. The only hope of ultimately suppressing slavery lay in the preservation of the Union, and every Abolitionist who argued or signed a petition for its dissolution was doing as much to perpetuate the evil he complained of as if he had been a slave-holder. The Liberty party, in running Birney, simply committed a political crime, evil in almost all its consequences; they in no sense paved the way for the Republican party, or helped forward the anti-slavery cause, or hurt the existing organizations. Their effect on the Democracy was *nil*; and all they were able to accomplish with the Whigs was to make them put forward for the ensuing campaign a slave-holder from Louisiana, with whom they were successful. Such were the remote results of their conduct; the immediate evils they produced have already been alluded to. They bore considerable resemblance—except that, after all, they really did have a principle to contend for—to the political prohibitionists of the present day, who go into the third party organizations, and are, not even excepting the saloon-keepers themselves, the most efficient allies on whom intemperance and the liquor traffic can count.

Anti-slavery men like Giddings, who supported Clay, were doing a thousand-fold more effective work for the cause they had at heart than all the voters who supported Birney; or, to speak more accurately, they were doing all they could to advance the cause, and the others were doing all they could to hold it back. Lincoln in 1860 occupied more nearly the ground held by Clay than that held by Birney; and the men who supported the latter in 1844 were the prototypes of those who wished to oppose Lincoln in 1860, and only worked less hard because they had less chance. The ultra Abolitionists discarded expediency, and claimed to act for abstract right, on principle, no matter what the results might be; in consequence they accomplished very little, and that as much for harm as for good, until they ate their words, went counter to their previous course, thereby acknowledging it to be bad, and supported in the Republican party the men and principles they had so fiercely condemned. The Liberty party was not in any sense the precursor of the Republican party, which was based as much on expediency as on abstract right, and was therefore able to accomplish good instead of harm. To say that the extreme Abolitionists triumphed in Republican success and were causes of it, is as absurd as it would be to call prohibitionists successful if, after countless futile efforts totally to prohibit the liquor traffic, and after savage denunciation of those who try to regulate it, they should then turn round and form a comparatively insignificant portion of a victorious high-license party.

Many people in speaking of the Abolitionists apparently forget that the national government, even under Republican rule, would never have meddled with slavery in the various states unless as a war measure, made necessary by the rebellion into which the South was led by a variety of causes, of which slavery was chief, but among which there were others that were also prominent; such as the separatist spirit of certain of the communities and the unscrupulous, treacherous ambition of such men as Davis, Floyd, and the rest. The Abolitionists' political organizations, such as the Liberty party, generally produced very little effect either way, and were scarcely thought of during the contests waged for freedom in Congress. The men who took a great and effective part in the fight against slavery were the men who remained within their respective parties; like the Democrats Benton and Wilmot, or the Whigs Seward and Stevens. When a new party with more clearly defined principles was formed, they, for the most part, went into it; but, like all other men who have ever had a really great influence, whether for good or bad, on American politics, they did not act independently of parties, but on the contrary kept within party lines,—although, of course, none of them were mere blind and unreasoning partisans.

The plea that slavery was a question of principle, on which no compromise could be accepted, might have been made and could still be made on twenty other points,—woman suffrage, for instance. Of course, to give women their just rights does not by any means imply that they should necessarily be allowed to vote, any more than the bestowal of the rights of citizenship upon blacks and aliens must of necessity carry with it the same privilege. But there were until lately, and in some states there are now, laws on the statute-book in reference to women that are in principle as unjust, and that are quite as much the remnants of archaic barbarism as was the old slave code; and though it is true that they do not work anything like the evil of the latter, they yet certainly work evil enough. The same laws that in one Southern state gave a master a right to whip a slave also allowed him to whip his wife, provided he used a stick no thicker than his little finger; the legal permission to do the latter was even more outrageous than that to do the former, yet no one considered it a ground for wishing a dissolution of the Union or for declaring against the existing parties. The folly of voting the Liberty ticket in 1844 differed in degree, but not at all in kind, from the folly of voting the Woman Suffrage ticket in 1884.

The intrigue for the annexation of Texas, and for thereby extending the slave territory of the Union, had taken shape towards the close of Tyler's term of office, while Calhoun was secretary of state. Benton, as an aggressive Western man, desirous of seeing our territorial possessions extended in any direction, north or south, always hoped that in the end Texas might be admitted into the Union; but he disliked seeing any premature steps taken, and was no party to the scheme of forcing an immediate annexation in the interests of slavery. Such immediate annexation was certain, among other things, to bring us into grave difficulties not only with Mexico, but also with England, which was strongly inclined to take much interest of a practical sort in the fate of Texas, and would, of course, have done all it could to bring about the abolition of slavery in that state. The Southerners, desirous of increasing the slave domain, and always in a state of fierce alarm over the proximity of any free state that might excite a servile insurrection, were impatient to add the Lone Star Republic of the Rio Grande to the number of their states; the Southwesterners fell in with them, influenced, though less strongly, by the same motives, and also by the lust for new lands and by race hatred towards the Mexicans and traditional jealousy of Great Britain; and these latter motives induced many Northwesterners to follow suit. By a judicious harping on all these strings Jackson himself, whose name was still a mighty power among the masses, was induced to write a letter favoring instant and prompt annexation.

This letter was really procured for political purposes. Tyler had completely identified himself with the Democracy, and especially with its extreme separatist wing, to which Calhoun also belonged, and which had grown so as to be already almost able to take the reins. The separatist chiefs were intriguing for the presidency, and were using annexation as a cry that would help them; and, failing in this attempt, many of the leaders were willing to break up the Union, and turn the Southern States, together with Texas, into a slave-holding confederacy. After Benton, the great champion of the old-style Union Democrats was Van Buren, who was opposed to immediate annexation, sharing the feeling that prevailed throughout the Northeast generally; although in certain circles all through the country there were men at work in its favor, largely as a mere matter of jobbery and from base motives, on account of speculations in Texan land and scrip, into which various capitalists and adventurers had gone rather extensively. Jackson, though a Southerner, warmly favored Van Buren, and was bitterly opposed to separatists; but the latter, by cunningly working on his feelings, without showing their own hands, persuaded him to write the letter mentioned, and promptly used it to destroy the chances of Van Buren, who was the man they chiefly feared; and though Jackson, at last roused to what was going on, immediately announced himself as in favor of Van Buren's candidacy, it was too late to undo the mischief.

Benton showed on this, as on many other occasions, much keener political ideas than his great political chief. He was approached by a politician, who himself was either one of those concerned in the presidential intrigues, or else one of their dupes, and who tried to win him over to take the lead on their side, complimenting him upon his former services to the cause of territorial expansion towards the southwest. Ordinarily the great Missourian was susceptible enough to such flattery; but on this occasion, preoccupied with the idea of an intrigue for the presidency, and indignant that there should be an effort made to implicate him in it, especially as it was mixed up with schemes of stock-jobbing and of disloyalty to the Union, he took fire at once, and answered with hot indignation, in words afterwards highly resented by his questioner, "that it was on the part of some an intrigue for the presidency, and a plot to dissolve the Union; on the part of others, a Texas scrip and land speculation; and that he was against it." The answer was published in the papers, and brought about a total break between Benton and the annexation party.

He was now thoroughly on the alert, and actively opposed at all points the schemes of those whom he regarded as concerned in or instigating the intrigue. He commented harshly on Tyler's annual message, which made a strong plea for annexation, even at the cost of a war both with Great Britain and Mexico; also on Calhoun's letter to Lord Aberdeen, which was certainly a remarkable diplomatic document,—being a thesis on slavery and the benefits resulting from it. Tyler's object was to prepare the way for a secret treaty, which should secure the desired object. Benton, in the course of some severe strictures on his acts, said, very truly, that it was evidently the intention to keep the whole matter as secret as possible until the treaty was concluded, "and then to force its adoption for the purpose of increasing the area of slave territory, or to make its rejection a cause for the secession of the Southern States; and in either event and in all cases to make the question of annexation a controlling one in the nomination of presidential candidates, and also in the election itself."

When the treaty proposed by the administration was rejected, and when it became evident that neither Tyler nor Calhoun, the two most prominent champions of the extreme separatists, had any chance for the Democratic nomination, the disunion side of the intrigue was brought to the front in many of the Southern States, beginning of course with South Carolina. A movement was made for a convention of the Southern States, to be held in the interest of the scheme; the key-note being struck in the cry of "Texas or disunion!" But this convention was given up, on account of the strong opposition it excited in the so-called "Border States,"—an opposition largely stirred up and led by Benton. Once more the haughty slave leaders of the Southeast had found that in the Missouri Senator they had an opponent whose fearlessness quite equaled their own, and whose stubborn temper and strength of purpose made him at least a match for themselves, in spite of all their dash and fiery impetuosity. It must have sounded strange, indeed, to Northern ears, accustomed to the harsh railings and insolent threats of the South Carolina senators, to hear one of the latter complaining that Benton's tone in the debate was arrogant, overbearing, and dictatorial towards those who were opposed to him. This same Senator, McDuffie, had been speaking of the proposed Southern meeting at Nashville; and Benton warned him that such a meeting would never take place, and that he had mistaken the temper of the Tennesseans; and also reminded him that General Jackson was still alive, and that the South Carolinians in particular must needs be careful if they hoped to agree with his followers, whose name was still legion, because he would certainly take the same position towards a disunion movement in the interests of slavery that he had already taken towards a nullification movement in the interests of free trade. "Preservation of the federal Union is as strong in the old Roman's heart now as ever; and while, as a Christian, he forgives all that is past (if it were past), yet no old tricks under new names! Texas disunion will be to him the same as tariff disunion; and if he detects a Texas disunionist nestling into his bed, I say again: Woe unto the luckless wight!" Boldly and forcibly he went on to paint the real motives of the promoters of the scheme, and the real character of the scheme itself; stating that, though mixed up with various speculative enterprises and with other intrigues, yet disunion was at the bottom of it all, and that already the cry had become, "Texas without the Union, rather than the Union without Texas!" "Under the pretext of getting Texas into the Union the scheme is to get the South out of it. A Southern Confederacy stretching from the Atlantic to the Californias ... is the cherished vision of disappointed ambition." He bitterly condemned secession, as simply disunion begat by nullification, and went on to speak of his own attitude in apparently opposing the admission of Texas, which he had always desired to see become a part of the Union, and which he had always insisted rightfully belonged to us, and to have been given away by Monroe's treaty with Spain. "All that is intended and foreseen. The intrigue for the presidency was the first act in the drama; the dissolution of the Union the second. And I, who hate intrigue and love the Union, can only speak of the intriguers and disunionists with warmth and indignation. The oldest advocate for the recovery of Texas, I must be allowed to speak in just terms of the criminal politicians who prostituted the question of its recovery to their own base purposes, and delayed its success by degrading and disgracing it. A Western man, and coming from a state more than any other interested in the recovery of this country, so unaccountably thrown away by the treaty of 1819, I must be allowed to feel indignant at seeing Atlantic politicians seizing upon it, and making it a sectional question for the purposes of ambition and disunion. I have spoken warmly of these plotters and intriguers; but I have not permitted their conduct to alter my own, or to relax my zeal for the recovery of the sacrificed country. I have helped to reject the disunion treaty; and that obstacle being removed, I have brought in the bill which will insure the recovery of Texas, with peace and honor, and with the Union."

It is important to remember, in speaking of his afterwards voting to admit Texas, that this was what he had all along favored, and that he now opposed it only on account of special circumstances. In both cases he was right; for, slavery or no slavery, it would have been a most unfortunate thing for us, and still worse for the Texans, if the latter had been allowed to develop into an independent nation. Benton deserves the greatest credit for the way in which he withstood the ignorant popular feeling of his own section in regard to Tyler's proposed treaty; and not only did he show himself able to withstand pressure from behind him, but also prompt in resenting threats made by outsiders. When McDuffie told him that the remembrance of his attitude on the bill would, to his harm, meet him on some future day, like the ghost that appeared to Brutus at Philippi, he answered:—

> I can promise the ghost and his backers that if the fight goes
> against me at this new Philippi, with which I am threatened,
> and the enemies of the American Union triumph over me
> as the enemies of Roman liberty triumphed over Brutus and
> Cassius, I shall not fall upon my sword, as Brutus did,
> though Cassius be killed, and run it through my own body;
> but I shall save it and save myself for another day and
> another use,—for the day when the battle of the disunion
> of these states is to be fought, not with words but with iron,
> and for the hearts of the traitors who appear in arms against
> their country.

Such a stern, defiant, almost prophetic warning did more to help the Union cause than volumes of elaborate constitutional argument, and it would have been well for the Northern States had they possessed men as capable of uttering it as was the iron Westerner. Benton always showed at his best when the honor or integrity of the nation was menaced, whether by foes from without or by foes from within. On such occasions his metal always rang true. When there was any question of breaking faith with the Union, or of treachery towards it, his figure always loomed up as one of the chief in the ranks of its defenders; and his follies and weaknesses sink out of sight when we think of the tremendous debt which the country owes him for his sorely tried and unswerving loyalty.

The treaty alluded to by Benton in his speech against the abortive secession movement was the one made with Texas while Calhoun was secretary of state, and submitted to the Senate by Tyler, with a message as extraordinary as some of his secretary's utterances. The treaty was preposterously unjust and iniquitous. It provided for the annexation of Texas, and also of a very large portion of Mexico, to which Texas had no possible title, and this without consulting Mexico in any way whatever; Calhoun advancing the plea that it was necessary to act immediately on account of the danger that Texas was in of falling under the control of England, and therefore having slavery abolished within its borders; while Tyler blandly announced that we had acquired title to the ceded territory—which belonged to one power and was ceded to us by another—through his signature to the treaty, and that, pending its ratification by the Senate, he had dispatched troops to the scene of action to protect the ceded land "from invasion,"—the territory to be thus protected from Mexican invasion being then and always having been part and parcel of Mexico.

Benton opposed the ratification of the treaty in a very strong speech, during which he mercilessly assailed both Tyler and Calhoun. The conduct of the former he dismissed with the contemptuous remark that he had committed "a caper about equal to the mad freaks with which the unfortunate Emperor Paul, of Russia, was accustomed to astonish Europe;" and roughly warned him to be careful how he tried to imitate Jackson's methods, because in heroic imitations there was no middle ground, and if he failed to fill the rôle of hero he would then perforce find himself playing that of harlequin. Calhoun received more attention, for he was far more worthy of a foeman's steel than was his nominal superior, and Benton exposed at length the willful exaggeration and the perversion of the truth of which the Carolinian had been guilty in trying to raise the alarm of English interference in Texas, for the purpose of excusing the haste with which the treaty was carried through.

He showed at length the outrage we should inflict upon Mexico by seizing "two thousand miles of her territory, without a word of explanation with her, and by virtue of a treaty with Texas to which she was no party;" and he conclusively proved, making use of his own extensive acquaintance with history, especially American history, that the old Texas, the only territory that the Texans themselves or we could claim with any shadow of right, made but a fraction of the territory now "ceded" to us. He laughed at the idea of calling the territory Texas, and speaking of its forcible cutting off as re-annexation, "Humboldt calls it New Mexico, Chihuahua, Coahuila and Nuevo Santander; and the civilized world may qualify this *re*-annexation by some odious and terrible epithet ... robbery;" then he went on to draw a biting contrast between our treatment of Mexico and our treatment of England. "Would we take two thousand miles of Canada in the same way? I presume not. And why not? Why not treat Great Britain and Mexico alike? Why not march up to 'fifty-four forty' as courageously as we march upon the Rio Grande? Because Great Britain is powerful and Mexico weak,—a reason which may fail in policy as much as in morals." Also he ridiculed the flurry of fear into which the Southern slave-holders affected to be cast by the dread of England's hostility to slavery, when they had just acquiesced in making a treaty with her by which we bound ourselves to help to put down the slave-trade. He then stated his own position, showing why he wished us to have the original Texan lands, if we could get them honorably, and without robbing Mexico of new territory; and at the same time sneered at Calhoun and Tyler because they had formerly favored the Monroe treaty, by which we abandoned our claims to them:—

> We want Texas, that is to say, the Texas of La Salle; and we want it for great natural reasons, obvious as day, and permanent as nature. We want it because it is geographically appurtenant to our division of North America, essential to our political, commercial, and social system, and because it would be detrimental and injurious to us to have it fall into the hands or sink under the domination of any foreign power. For these reasons I was against sacrificing the country when it was thrown away,—and thrown away by those who are now so suddenly possessed of a fury to get it back. For these reasons I am for getting it back whenever it can be done with peace and honor, or even at the price of just war against any intrusive European power; but I am against all disguise and artifice,—against all pretexts,—and especially against weak and groundless pretexts, discreditable to ourselves and offensive to others, too thin and shallow not to be seen through by every beholder, and merely invented to cover unworthy purposes.

The treaty was rejected by an overwhelming vote, although Buchanan led a few of his timeserving comrades from the North to the support of the extreme Southern element. Benton then tried, but failed, to get through a bill providing for a joint agreement between Mexico, Texas, and the United States to settle definitely all boundary questions. Meanwhile the presidential election occurred, with the result already mentioned. The separatist and annexationist Democrats, the extreme slavery wing of the party, defeated Van Buren and nominated Polk, who was their man; the Whigs nominated Clay, who was heartily opposed to all the schemes of the disunion and extreme slavery men, and who, if elected, while he might very properly have consented to the admission of Texas with its old boundaries, would never have brought on a war nor have attempted to add a vast extent of new slave territory to the Union. Clay would have been elected, and the slavery disunionists defeated, if in the very nick of time the Abolitionists had not stepped in to support the latter, and by their blindness in supporting Birney given the triumph to their own most bitter opponents. Then the Abolitionists, having played their only card, and played it badly, had to sit still and see what evil their acts had produced; they had accomplished just as much as men generally do accomplish when they dance to the tune that their worst foes play.

Polk's election gave an enormous impulse to the annexation movement, and made it doubly and trebly difficult for any one to withstand it. The extreme disunion and slavery men, of course, hated Benton, himself a Southwesterner from a slave-holding state, with peculiar venom, on account of his attitude, very justly regarding him as the main obstacle in their path; and the din and outcry raised against all who opposed the schemes of the intriguers was directed with especial fury against the Missourian. He was accused of being allied to the Whigs, of wishing to break up the Democracy, and of many other things. Indeed, Benton's own people were very largely against him, and it must always be remembered that whereas Northeastern statesmen were certain to be on the popular side in taking a stand against the extreme pro-slavery men, Benton's position was often just the reverse. With them it was politic to do right; with him it was not; and for this reason the praise awarded the latter should be beyond measure greater than that awarded to the former.

Still, there can be little question that he was somewhat, even although only slightly, influenced by the storm of which he had to bear the brunt; indeed, he would have been more than human if he had not been; and probably this outside pressure was one among the causes that induced him to accept a compromise in the matter, which took effect just before Polk was inaugurated. The House of Representatives had passed a resolution giving the consent of Congress to the admission of Texas as a state, and allowing it the privilege of forming four additional states out of its territory, whenever it should see fit. The line of the Missouri Compromise, 36° 30', was run through this new territory, slavery being prohibited in the lands lying north of it, and permissible or not, according to the will of the state seeking admission, in those lying south of it. Benton meanwhile had introduced a bill merely providing that negotiations should be entered into with Texas for its admission, the proposed treaty or articles of agreement to be submitted to the Senate or to Congress. He thereby kept the control in the hands of the legislature, which the joint resolution did not; and moreover, as he said in his speech, he wished to provide for due consideration being shown Mexico in the arrangement of the boundary, and for the matter being settled by commissioners.

Neither resolution nor bill could get through by itself; and accordingly it was proposed to combine both into one measure, leaving the president free to choose either plan. To this proposition Benton finally consented, it being understood that, as only three days of Tyler's term remained, the execution of the act would be left to the incoming president, and that the latter would adopt Benton's plans. The friends of the admission of Texas assured the doubtful voters that such would be the case. Polk himself gave full assurance that he would appoint a commission, as provided by Benton's bill, if passed, with the House resolution as an alternative; and McDuffie, Calhoun's friend, and the senator from South Carolina, announced without reserve that Calhoun—for Tyler need not be considered in the matter, after it had been committed to the great nullifier—would not have the "audacity" to try to take the settlement of the question away from the president, who was to be inaugurated on the fourth of March. On the strength of these assurances, which, if made good, would, of course, have rendered the "alternative" a merely nominal one, Benton supported the measure, which was then passed. Contrary to all expectation, Calhoun promptly acted upon the legislative clause, and Polk made no effort to undo what the former had done. This caused intense chagrin and anger to the Bentonians; but they should certainly have taken such a contingency into account, and though they might with much show of reason say that they had been tricked into acting as they had done, yet it is probable that the immense pressure from behind had made Benton too eager to follow any way he could find that would take him out of the position into which his conscience had led him. No amount of pressure would have made him deliberately sanction a wrong; but it did render him a little less wary in watching to see that the right was not infringed upon. It was most natural that he should be anxious to find a common ground for himself and his constituents to stand on; but it is to be regretted that this anxiety to find a common ground should have made him willing to trust blindly to vague pledges and promises, which he ought to have known would not be held in the least binding by those on whose behalf they were supposed to be made.

Acting under this compromise measure Texas was admitted, and the foundation for our war with Mexico was laid. Calhoun, under whom this was done, nevertheless sincerely regretted the war itself, and freely condemned Polk's administration for bringing it on; his own position being that he desired to obtain without a war what it was impossible we should get except at the cost of one. Benton, who had all along consistently opposed doing a wrong to Mexico, attacked the whole war party, and in a strong and bitter speech accused Calhoun of being the cause of the contest; showing plainly that, whatever the ex-secretary of state might say in regard to the acts immediately precipitating the conflict, he himself was responsible as being in truth their original cause. While stating his conviction, however, that Calhoun was the real author of the war, Benton added that he did not believe that war was his object, although an inevitable incident of the course he had pursued.

Although heartily opposed to the war in its origin, Benton very properly believed in prosecuting it with the utmost vigor when once we were fairly in; and it was mainly owing to him that the proposed policy of a "masterly inactivity" was abandoned, and the scheme of pushing straight for the city of Mexico adopted in its stead. Indeed, it was actually proposed to make him lieutenant-general, and therefore the commander-in-chief of our forces in Mexico; but this was defeated in the Senate, very fortunately, as it would have been a great outrage upon Scott, Taylor, and every other soldier with real military training. It seems extraordinary that Benton himself should not have seen the absurdity and wrong of such a proposition.

The wonderful hardihood and daring shown in the various expeditions against Mexico, especially in those whereby her northwest territory was wrested from her, naturally called forth all Benton's sympathy; and one of his best speeches was that made to welcome Doniphan's victorious volunteers after their return home from their famous march to Chihuahua.

CHAPTER XIV.

SLAVERY IN THE NEW TERRITORIES.

Hardly was Polk elected before it became evident to Benton and the other Jacksonians that the days of the old Union or Nationalist Democracy were over, and that the separatist and disunion elements within the party had obtained the upper hand. The first sign of the new order of things was the displacement of Blair, editor of the "Globe," the Democratic newspaper organ. Blair was a strong Unionist, and had been bitterly hostile to Calhoun and the Nullifiers. He had also opposed Tyler, the representative of those states-rights and separatist Democrats, who by their hostility to Jackson had been temporarily driven into the Whig camp, and who, finding themselves in very uncongenial society, and seeing, moreover, that their own principles were gradually coming to the front in the old party, had begun drifting back again into it. Polk's chances of election were so precarious that he was most anxious to conciliate the Separatists; besides which he at heart sympathized with their views, and had himself been brought forward in the Democratic convention to beat the National candidate, Van Buren. Moreover, Tyler withdrew from the contest in his favor; in part payment for which help, soon after the election, Blair was turned out, and Ritchie of Virginia, a man whose views suited the new Democratic leaders, was put in his place; to the indignation not only of Benton, but also of Jackson himself, then almost on his death-bed. Of course the break between the two wings was as yet by no means complete. Polk needed the Union Democrats, and the latter were still in good party standing. Benton himself, as has been seen, was offered the command of all the forces in Mexico, but the governmental policy, and the attitude of the party in Congress after 1844, were widely different from what they had been while Jackson's influence was supreme, or while the power he left behind him was wielded by a knot of Union men.

From this time the slavery question dwarfed all others, and was the one with which Benton, as well as other statesmen, had mainly to deal. He had been very loath to acknowledge that it was ever to become of such overshadowing importance; until late in his life he had not realized that, interwoven with the disunionist movement, it had grown so as to become in reality the one and only question before the people; but, this once thoroughly understood, he henceforth devoted his tremendous energies to the struggle with it. He possessed such phenomenal power of application and of study, and his capacity for and his delight in work were so extraordinary, that he was able at the same time to grapple with many other subjects of importance, and to present them in a way that showed he had thoroughly mastered them both in principle and detail,—as witness his speech in favor of giving the control of the coast survey to the navy; but henceforth the importance of his actions lay in their relation to the slavery extension movements.

He had now entered on what may fairly be called the heroic part of his career; for it would be difficult to choose any other word to express our admiration for the unflinching and defiant courage with which, supported only by conscience and by his loving loyalty to the Union, he battled for the losing side, although by so doing he jeopardized and eventually ruined his political prospects, being finally, as punishment for his boldness in opposing the dominant faction of the Missouri Democracy, turned out of the Senate, wherein he had passed nearly half his life. Indeed, his was one of those natures that show better in defeat than in victory. In his career there were many actions that must command our unqualified admiration; such were his hostility to the Nullifiers, wherein, taking into account his geographical location and his refusal to compromise, he did better than any other public man, not even excepting Jackson and Webster; his belief in honest money; and his attitude towards all questions involving the honor or the maintenance and extension of the Union. But in all these matters he was backed more or less heartily by his state, and he had served four terms in the federal Senate as the leading champion and representative, not alone of Missouri, but also of the entire West. When, however, the slavery question began to enter upon its final stage, Benton soon found himself opposed to a large and growing faction of the Missouri Democracy, which increased so rapidly that it soon became dominant. But he never for an instant yielded his convictions, even when he saw the ground being thus cut from under his feet, fighting for the right as sturdily as ever, facing his fate fearlessly, and going down without a murmur. The contrast between the conduct towards the slavery disunionists of this Democrat from a slave-holding state, with a hostile majority at home against him, and the conduct of Webster, a Whig, enthusiastically backed by his own free state, in the same issue, is a painful one for the latter. Indeed, on any moral point, Benton need have no cause to fear comparison with any of his great rivals in the political arena. During his career, the United States Senate was perhaps the most influential, and certainly the ablest legislative body in the world; and after Jackson's presidency came to an end the really great statesmen and political leaders of the country were to be found in it, and not in the executive chair. The period during which the great Missourian was so prominent a figure in our politics, and which lasted up to the time of the Civil War, might very appropriately be known in our history as the time of the supremacy of the Senate. Such senators as Benton, Webster, Clay, and Calhoun, and later on Douglas, Seward, and Sumner, fairly towered above presidents like the obscure Southerners, Tyler and Polk, or the truckling, timeserving Northern politicians, Pierce and Buchanan. During the long interval coming between the two heroic ages of American history,—the age of Washington and Franklin, and the age of Lincoln and Grant,—it was but rarely that the nation gave its greatest gift to its best or its greatest son.

Benton had come into the Senate at the same time that Missouri was admitted into the Union, with thanks, therefore, to the same measure, the Missouri Compromise bill. This shut out slavery from all territory north of the line of 36° 30', and did not make it obligatory even where it was permissible; and the immediate cause of Benton's downfall was his courage and persistency in defending the terms of this compromise from the attacks of the Southern slavery extensionists and disunionists. The pro-slavery feeling was running ever higher and higher throughout the South; and his stand on this question aroused the most furious anger among a constantly increasing number of his constituents, and made him the target for bitter and savage assaults on the part of his foes, the spirit of hostility against him being carried to such length as finally almost to involve him in an open brawl on the floor of the Senate with one of his colleagues, Foote, who, like his fellow fire-eaters, found that Benton was not a man who could be bullied. Indeed, his iron will and magnificent physique both fitted him admirably for such a contest against odds, and he seems to have entered into it with a positive zest.

The political Abolitionists having put Polk in power, their action bore fruit after its kind, and very soon the question had to be faced, as to what should be done with the immense tracts of territory conquered from Mexico. Benton opposed, as being needless and harmful, the Wilmot Proviso, which forbade the introduction of slavery into any part of the territory so acquired. He argued, and produced in evidence the laws and Constitution of Mexico, that the soil of California and Mexico was already free, and that as slavery would certainly never be, and indeed could never be, introduced into either territory, the agitation of the question could only result in harm. Calhoun and the other extreme slavery leaders welcomed the discussion over this proviso, which led Benton to remark that the Abolitionists and the Nullifiers were necessary to each other,—the two blades of a pair of shears, neither of which could cut until they were joined together.

When Calhoun introduced his famous resolutions declaring that Congress had no power to interfere with slavery in the territories, and therefore no power to prevent the admission of new states except on the condition of their prohibiting slavery within their limits, Benton promptly and strongly opposed them as being firebrands needlessly thrown to inflame the passions of the extremists, and, moreover, as being disunionist in tendency. The following is his own account of what then took place: "Mr. Calhoun said he had expected the support of Mr. Benton 'as the representative of a slave-holding state.' Mr. Benton answered that it was impossible that he could have expected such a thing. 'Then,' said Mr. Calhoun, 'I shall know where to find that gentleman.' To which Mr. Benton said: 'I shall be found in the right place,—on the side of my country and the Union.' This answer, given on that day and on the spot, is one of the incidents of his life which Mr. Benton will wish posterity to remember." We can easily pardon the vanity which wishes and hopes that such an answer, given under such conditions, may be remembered. Indeed, Benton's attitude throughout all this period should never be forgotten; and the words he spoke in answer to Calhoun marked him as the leader among those Southerners who held the nation above any section thereof, even their own, and whose courage and self-sacrifice in the cause of the Union entitled them to more praise than by right belongs to any equal number of Northerners; those Southerners who in the civil war furnished Farragut, Thomas, Bristow, and countless others as loyal as they were brave. The effect of Benton's teachings and the still remaining influence of his intense personality did more than aught else to keep Missouri within the Union, when her sister states went out of it.

Benton always regarded much of the slavery agitation in the South as being political in character, and the result of the schemes of ambitious and unscrupulous leaders. He believed that Calhoun had introduced a set of resolutions that were totally uncalled for, simply for the purpose of carrying a question to the Slave States on which they could be formed into a unit against the Free States; and there is much to be said in support of his view. Certainly the resolutions mark the beginning of the first great slavery agitation throughout the Southern States, which was engineered and guided for their own ends by politicians like Jefferson Davis. These resolutions were absolutely inconsistent with many of Calhoun's previous declarations; and that fact was also sharply commented on by Benton in his speeches and writings. He also criticised with caustic severity Calhoun's statements that he wished to save the Union by forcing the North to take a position so agreeable to the South as to make the latter willing not to separate. He showed that Calhoun's proposed "constitutional" and "peaceable" methods of bringing this about by prohibiting commercial intercourse between the two sections would themselves be flagrant breaches of the Constitution and acts of disunion,—all the more so as it was proposed to discriminate in favor of the Northwest as against the Northeast. Calhoun wished to bring about a convention of the Southern States, in order to secure the necessary unity of action; and one of the main obstacles to the success of the plan was Missouri's refusal to take part in it. Great efforts were made to win her over, and to beat down Benton; the extreme pro-slavery men honoring him with a hatred more intense than that they harbored towards any Northerner. Some of Calhoun's recent biographers have credited him with being really a Union man at heart. It seems absolutely impossible that this could have been the case; and the supposition is certainly not compatible with the belief that he retained his right senses. Benton characterizes his system of slavery agitation, very truthfully, as being one "to force issues upon the North under the pretext of self-defense, and to sectionalize the South, preparatory to disunion, through the instrumentality of sectional conventions, composed wholly of delegates from the slave-holding states."

When the question of the admission of Oregon came up, Calhoun attempted to apply to it a dogma wholly at variance with all his former positions on the subject. This was the theory of the self-extension of the slavery part of the Constitution to the territories; that is, he held that the exclusion of slavery from any part of the new territory was itself a subversion of the Constitution. Such a dogma was so monstrous in character, so illogical, so inconsistent with all his former theories, and so absolutely incompatible with the preservation of the Union, that it renders it impossible to believe that his asseverations of devotion to the latter were uttered honestly or in good faith. Most modern readers will agree with Benton that he deliberately worked to bring about secession.

Meanwhile the Missourian had gained an ally of his own stamp in the Senate. This was Houston, from the new State of Texas, who represented in that state, like Andrew Jackson in Tennessee, and Benton himself in Missouri, the old Nationalist Democracy, which held the preservation of the Union dear above all other things. Houston was a man after Benton's own heart, and was thoroughly Jacksonian in type. He was rough, honest, and fearless, a devoted friend and a vengeful enemy, and he promised that combination of stubborn courage and capacity of devotion to an ideal that renders a man an invaluable ally in a fight against odds for principle.

After much discussion and amendment, the Oregon bill, containing a radical anti-slavery clause, passed both houses and became a law in spite of the violent opposition of some of the Southerners, headed by Calhoun, who announced that the great strife between the North and the South was ended, and that the time had come for the South to show that, though she prized the Union, yet there were matters which she regarded as of greater importance than its preservation. His ire was most fiercely excited by the action of Benton and Houston in supporting the bill, and after his return to South Carolina he denounced them by name as traitors to the South,—"a denunciation," says Benton, "which they took for a distinction; as what he called treason to the South they knew to be allegiance to the Union." When it was proposed to extend by bill the Constitution of the United States into the territories, with a view to carrying slavery into California, Utah, and New Mexico, Benton was again opposed to Calhoun. As a matter of course, too, he was the stoutest opponent of the Southern convention and other similar disunion movements that were beginning to take shape throughout the South, instigated by the two rank secession states of South Carolina and Mississippi.

Most of the momentous questions springing out of the war with Mexico were left by Polk as legacies to his successor, when the former went out of office, after an administration that Benton criticised with extreme sharpness, although he tried to shield the president by casting the blame for his actions upon his cabinet advisers; characterizing the Mexican War as one of "speculation and intrigue," and as the "great blot" of his four years' term of office, and ridiculing the theory that we were acting in self-defense, or that our soil had been invaded. In 1848 the Democrats nominated Cass, a Northern pro-slavery politician of moderate abilities, and the Whigs put up and elected old Zachary Taylor, the rough frontier soldier and Louisiana slave-holder. The political Abolitionists again took a hand in the contest, but this time abandoned their abolition theories, substituting instead thereof the prohibition of slavery in the new territories. They derived much additional importance from their alliance with a disappointed politician in the pivotal State of New York; and in this case, in sharp contrast to the result in 1844, their actions worked good, and not evil. Van Buren, chagrined and angered by the way he was treated by the regular Democrats, organized a revolt against them, and used the banner of the new Free Soil party as one under which to rally his adherents. This movement was of consequence mainly in New York, and there it soon became little more than a mere fight between the two sections of the Democracy. Benton himself visited this all-important state to try to patch up matters, but he fortunately failed. The factions proved very nearly equal in strength; and as a consequence the Whigs carried the state and the election, and once more held the reins of government.

When a Louisiana slave-holder was thus installed in the White House, the extreme Southern men may have thought that they were sure of him as an ally in their fight against freedom. But, if so, they soon found they had reckoned without their host, for the election of Taylor affords a curious, though not solitary, instance in which the American people builded better than they knew in choosing a chief executive. Nothing whatever was known of his political theories, and the Whigs nominated him simply because he was a successful soldier, likely to take the popular fancy. But once elected he turned out to have the very qualities we then most needed in a president,— a stout heart, shrewd common sense, and thorough-going devotion to the Union. Although with widely different training from Benton, and nominally differing from him in politics, he was yet of the same stamp both in character and principles; both were Union Southerners, not in the least afraid of openly asserting their opinions, and, if necessary, of making them good by their acts. In his first and only annual message, Taylor expressed, upon all the important questions of the day, views that were exactly similar to those advanced before or after by Benton himself in the Senate; and he used similar emphasis and plainness of speech. He declared the Union to be the greatest of blessings, which he would maintain in every way against whatever dangers might threaten it; he advised the admission of California, which wished to come in as a free state; he thought that the territories of Utah and New Mexico should be left as they were; and he warned the Texans, who were blustering about certain alleged rights to New Mexican soil, and threatening to take them by force of arms, that this could not be permitted, and that the matter would have to be settled by the judicial authority of the United States. Benton heartily indorsed the message. Naturally, it was bitterly assailed by the disunionists under Calhoun; and even Clay, who entirely lacked Taylor's backbone, was dissatisfied with it as being too extreme in tone, and conflicting with his proposed compromise measures. These same compromise measures brought the Kentucky leader into conflict with Benton also, especially on the point of their interfering with the immediate admission of California into the Union.

This is not the place to discuss Clay's proposed compromise, which was not satisfactory to the extreme Southerners, and still less so to the Unionists and anti-slavery men. It consisted of five different parts, relating to the recovery of fugitive slaves, the suppression of the slave-trade in the District of Columbia, the admission of California as a state, and the territorial condition of Utah and New Mexico. Benton opposed it as mixing up incongruous measures; as being unjust to California, inasmuch as it confounded the question of her admission with the general slavery agitation in the United States; and above all as being a concession or capitulation to the spirit of disunion and secession, and therefore a repetition of the error of 1833. Benton always desired to meet and check any disunion movement at the very outset, and, if he had had his way, would have carried matters with a high hand whenever it came to dealing with threats of such a proceeding; and therein he was perfectly right. In regard to the proposed compromise he believed in dealing with each question as it arose, beginning with the admission of California, and refusing to have any compromise at all with those who threatened secession.

The slavery extensionists endeavored to have the Missouri compromise line stretched on to the Pacific. Benton, avowing his belief that slavery was an evil, opposed this, and gave his reasons why he did not wish to see the line which had been used to divide free and slave soil in the French or Louisiana purchase extended into the lands won from Mexico. Slavery had always existed in Louisiana, while it had been long abolished in Mexico. "The Missouri compromise line, extending to New Mexico and California, though astronomically the same as that in Louisiana, would be politically directly the opposite. One went through a territory all slave, and made one half free; the other would go through territory all free, and make one half slave." In fact Benton, as he grew older, unlike most of his compatriots, gained a clearer insight into the effects of slavery. This was shown in his comments upon

Calhoun's statement, made in the latter's last speech, in reference to the unequal development of the North and South; which, Benton said, was partly owing to the existence of "slavery itself, which he (Calhoun) was so anxious to extend." It was in this same speech that Calhoun hinted at his plan for a dual executive,—one president from the Free and one from the Slave States,—a childish proposition, that Benton properly treated as a simple absurdity.

In his speech against the compromise, Benton discussed it, section by section, with great force, and with his usual blunt truthfulness. His main count was the injustice done to California by delaying her admittance, and making it dependent upon other issues; but he made almost as strong a point against the effort to settle the claims of Texas to New Mexican territory. The Texan threats to use force he treated with cavalier indifference, remarking that as long as New Mexico was a territory, and therefore belonged to the United States, any controversy with her was a controversy with the federal government, which would know how to play her part by "defending her territory from invasion, and her people from violence,"—a hint that had a salutary effect upon the Texans; in fact the disunionists, generally, were not apt to do much more than threaten while a Whig like Taylor was backed up by a Democrat like Benton. He also pointed out that it was not necessary, however desirable, to make a compact with Texas about the boundaries, as they could always be settled, whether she wished it or not, by a suit before the Supreme Court; and again intimated that a little show of firmness would remove all danger of a collision. "As to anything that Texas or New Mexico may do in taking or relinquishing possession, that is all moonshine. New Mexico is the property of the United States, and she cannot dispose of herself or any part of herself, nor can Texas take her or any part of her." He showed a thorough acquaintance with New Mexican geography and history, and alluded to the bills he had already brought in, in 1844 and 1850, to establish a divisional line between the territory and Texas, on the longitude first of one hundred and then of one hundred and two degrees. He recalled the fact that before the annexation of Texas, and in a bill proposing to settle all questions with her, he had inserted a provision forever prohibiting slavery in all parts of the annexed territory lying west of the hundredth degree of longitude. He also took the opportunity of formally stating his opposition to any form of slavery extension, remarking that it was no new idea with him, but dated from the time when in 1804, while a law student in Tennessee, he had studied Blackstone as edited by the learned Virginian, Judge Tucker, who, in an appendix, treated of, and totally condemned, black slavery in the United States. The very difficulty, or, as he deemed it, the impossibility, of getting rid of the evil, made Benton all the more determined in opposing its extension. "The incurability of the evil is the greatest objection to the extension of slavery. If it is wrong for the legislator to inflict an evil which can be cured, how much more to inflict one that is incurable, and against the will of the people who are to endure it forever! I quarrel with no one for deeming slavery a blessing; I deem it an evil, and would neither adopt it nor impose it on others." The solution of the problem of disposing of existent slavery, he confessed, seemed beyond human wisdom; but "there is a wisdom above human, and to that we must look. In the mean time, do not extend the evil." In justification of his position he quoted previous actions of Congress, done under the lead of Southern men, in refusing again and again, down to 1807, to allow slavery to be introduced into Indiana, when that community petitioned for it. He also repudiated strongly the whole spirit in which Clay had gotten up his compromise bill, stating that he did not believe in geographical parties; that he knew no North and no South, and utterly rejected any slavery compromises except those to be found in the Constitution. Altogether it was a great speech, and his opposition was one of the main causes of the defeat of Clay's measure.

Benton's position on the Wilmot Proviso is worth giving in his own words: "That measure was rejected again as heretofore, and by the votes of those who were opposed to extending slavery into the territories, because it was unnecessary and inoperative,—irritating to the Slave States, without benefit to the Free States, a mere work of supererogation, of which the fruit was discontent. It was rejected, not on the principle of non-intervention; not on the principle of leaving to the territories to do as they pleased on the question, but because there had been intervention; because Mexican law and constitution had intervened, had abolished slavery by law in those dominions; which law would remain in force until repealed by Congress. All that the opponents to the extension of slavery had to do, then, was to do nothing. And they did nothing."

Before California was admitted into the Union old Zachary Taylor had died, leaving behind him a name that will always be remembered among our people. He was neither a great statesman nor yet a great commander; but he was an able and gallant soldier, a loyal and upright public servant, and a most kindly, honest, and truthful man. His death was a greater loss to the country than perhaps the people ever knew.

The bill for the admission of California as a free state, heartily sustained by Benton, was made a test question by the Southern disunionists; but on this occasion they were thoroughly beaten. The great struggle was made over a proposition to limit the southern boundary of the state to the line of 36° 30', and to extend the Missouri line through to the Pacific, so as to authorize the existence of slavery in all the territory south of that latitude. This was defeated by a vote of thirty-two to twenty-four. Not only Benton, but also Spruance and Wales of Delaware, and Underwood of Kentucky, joined with the representatives from the Free States in opposing it. Had it not been for the action of these four slave-state senators in leaving their associates, the vote would have been a tie; and their courage and patriotism should be remembered. The bill was then passed by a vote of thirty-four to eighteen, two other Southern senators, Houston of Texas, and Bell of Tennessee, voting for it, in addition to the four already mentioned. After its passage, ten of the senators who had voted against it, including, of course, Jefferson Davis, and also Benton's own colleague from Missouri, Atchison, joined in a protest against what had been done, ending with a thinly veiled threat of disunion,—"dissolution of the confederacy," as they styled it. Benton stoutly and successfully opposed allowing this protest to be received or entered upon the journal, condemning it, with a frankness that very few of his fellow-senators would have dared to copy, as being sectional and disunion in form, and therefore unfit even for preservation on the records.

When the Fugitive Slave Act of 1850 was passed, through the help of some Northern votes, Benton refused to support it; and this was the last act of importance that he performed as United States Senator. He had risen and grown steadily all through his long term of service; and during its last period he did greater service to the nation than any of his fellow-senators. Compare his stand against the slavery extremists and disunionists, such as Calhoun, with the position of Webster at the time of his famous seventh of March speech, or with that of Clay when he brought in his compromise bill! In fact, as the times grew more troublesome, he grew steadily better able to do good work in them.

It is this fact of growth that especially marks his career. No other American statesman, except John Quincy Adams,—certainly neither of his great contemporaries, Webster and Clay,—kept doing continually better work throughout his term of public service, or showed himself able to rise to a higher level at the very end than at the beginning. Yet such was the case with Benton. He always rose to meet a really great emergency; and his services to the nation grew steadily in importance to the very close of his life. Whereas Webster and Clay passed their zenith and fell, he kept rising all the time.

CHAPTER XV.

THE LOSING FIGHT.

Benton had now finished his fifth and last term in the United States Senate. He had been chosen senator from Missouri before she was admitted into the Union, and had remained such for thirty years. During all that time the state had been steadily Democratic, the large Whig minority never being able to get control; but on the question of the extension of slavery the dominant party itself began at this time to break into two factions. Hitherto Benton had been the undisputed leader of the Democracy, but now the pro-slavery and disunionist Democrats organized a very powerful opposition to him; while he still received the enthusiastic support of an almost equally numerous body of followers. Although the extension of slavery and the preservation of the Union were the two chief and vital points on which the factions differed, yet the names by which they designated each other were adopted in consequence of their differing also on a third and only less important one. Benton was such a firm believer in hard money, and a currency of gold and silver, as to have received the nickname of "Old Bullion," and his followers were called "hards;" his opponents were soft money men, in addition to being secessionists and pro-slavery fanatics, and took the name of "softs." The principles of the Bentonians were right, and those of their opponents wrong; but for all that the latter gradually gained upon the former. Finally, in the midst of Benton's fight against the extension of slavery into the territories, the "softs" carried the Missouri legislature, and passed a series of resolutions based upon those of Calhoun. These were most truculent and disloyal in tone, demanding that slavery be permitted to exist in all the new states to be admitted, and instructing their senators to vote accordingly. These resolutions were presented in the senate by Benton's colleague from Missouri, Atchison, who was rather hostile to him and to every other friend of the Union, and later on achieved disreputable notoriety as a leader of the "border ruffians" in the affrays on the soil of Kansas. Benton at once picked up the glove that had been flung down. He utterly refused to obey the resolutions, denounced them savagely as being treasonable and offensive in the highest degree, asserted that they did not express the true opinions of the voters of the state, and appealed from the Missouri legislature to the Missouri people.

The issue between the two sides was now sharply brought out, and, as this took place towards the end of Benton's fifth term, the struggle to command the legislature which should reëlect him or give him a successor was most exciting. Benton himself took an active part in the preliminary canvass. Neither faction was able to get a majority of the members, and the deadlock was finally broken by the "softs" coming to the support of the Whigs, and helping them to elect Benton's rival. Thus, after serving his state faithfully and ably for thirty years, he was finally turned out of the position which he so worthily filled, because he had committed the crime of standing loyally by the Union.

But the stout old Nationalist was not in the least cast down or even shaken by his defeat. He kept up the fight as bitterly as ever, though now an old man, and in 1852 went to Congress as a representative Union Democrat. For thirty years he had been the autocrat of Missouri politics, and had at one time wielded throughout his own state a power as great as Calhoun possessed in South Carolina; greater than Webster held in Massachusetts, or Clay in Kentucky. But the tide which had so long flowed in his favor now turned, and for the few remaining years of his life set as steadily against him; yet at no time of his long public career did he stand forth as honorably and prominently as during his last days, when he was showing so stern a front to his victorious foes. His love for work was so great that, when out of the Senate, he did not find even his incessant political occupations enough for him. During his contest for the senatorship his hands had been full, for he had spoken again and again throughout the entire state, his carefully prepared speeches showing remarkable power, and filled with scathing denunciation and invective and biting and caustic sarcasm. But so soon as his defeat was assured he turned his attention immediately to literature, setting to work on his great "Thirty Years' View," of which the first volume was printed during his congressional term, and was quoted on the floor of the House, both by his friends and foes, during the debates in which he was taking part.

In 1852, when he was elected to Congress as a member of the House, he had supported Pierce for the presidency against Scott, a good general, but otherwise a wholly absurd and flatulent personage, who was the Whig nominee. But it soon became evident that Pierce was completely under the control of the secession wing of the party, and Benton thereafterwards treated him with contemptuous hostility, despising him, and seeing him exactly as he was,—a small politician, of low capacity and mean surroundings, proud to act as the servile tool of men worse than himself but also stronger and abler. He was ever ready to do any work the slavery leaders set him, and to act as their attorney in arguing in its favor,—to quote Benton's phrase, with "undaunted mendacity, moral callosity [and] mental obliquity." His last message to Congress in the slavery interest Benton spoke of as characteristic, and exemplifying "all the modes of conveying untruths which long ages have invented,—direct assertion, fallacious inference, equivocal phrase, and false innuendo." As he entertained such views of the head of the Democratic party, and as this same head was in hearty accord with, and a good representative of the mass of the rank and file politicians of the organization, it is small wonder that Benton found himself, on every important question that came up while he was in Congress, opposed to the mass of his fellow-Democrats.

Although the great questions to which he devoted himself, while a representative in Congress, were those relating to the extension of slavery, yet he also found time to give to certain other subjects, working as usual with indomitable energy, and retaining his marvelous memory to the last. The idea of desponding or giving up, for any cause whatever, simply never entered his head. When his house, containing all the manuscript and papers of the nearly completed second volume of his "Thirty Years' View," was burned up, he did not delay a minute in recommencing his work, and the very next day spoke in Congress as usual.

His speeches were showing a steady improvement; they were not masterpieces, even at the last, but in every way, especially in style, they were infinitely superior to those that he had made on his first entrance into public life. Of course, a man with his intense pride in his country, and characterized by such a desire to see her become greater and more united in every way, would naturally support the proposal to build a Pacific Railroad, and accordingly he argued for it at great length and with force and justness, at the same time opposing the propositions to build northern and southern trans-continental roads as substitutes for the proposed central route. He showed the character of the land through which the road would run, and the easiness of the passes across the Rockies, and prophesied a rapid increase of states as one of the results attendant upon its building. At the end of his speech he made an elaborate comparison of the courses of trade and commerce at different periods of the world's history, and showed that, as we had reached the Pacific coast, we had finally taken a position where our trade with the Oriental kingdoms, backed up by our own enormous internal development, rendered us more than ever independent of Europe.

In another speech he discussed very intelligently, and with his usual complete command of the facts of the case, some of the contemporary Indian uprisings in the far West. He attacked our whole Indian policy, showing that the corruption of the Indian agents, coupled with astute aggressions, were the usual causes of our wars. Further, he criticised our regular troops as being unfit to cope with the savages, and advocated the formation of companies of frontier rangers, who should also be settlers, and should receive from the government a bounty in land as part reward for their service. Many of his remarks on our Indian policy apply quite as well now as they did then, and our regular soldiers are certainly not the proper opponents for the Indians; but Benton's military views were, as a rule, the reverse of sensible, and we cannot accept his denunciations of the army, and especially of West Point, as being worth serious consideration. His belief in the marvelous efficacy of a raw militia, especially as regards war with European powers, was childish, and much of his feeling against the regular army officer was dictated by jealousy. He was, by all the peculiarities of his habits and education, utterly unfitted for military command; and it would have been an evil day for his good fame if Polk had succeeded in having him made lieutenant-general of our forces in Mexico.

His remarks upon our Indian policy were not the only ones he made that would bear study even yet. Certain of his speeches upon the different land-bounty and pension bills, passed nominally in the interests of veterans, but really through demagogy and the machination of speculators, could be read with profit by not a few Congressmen at the present time. One of his utterances was: "I am a friend to old soldiers ... but not to old speculators;" and while favoring proper pension bills he showed the foolishness and criminality of certain others very clearly, together with the fact that, when passed long after the services have been rendered, they always fail to relieve the real sufferers, and work in the interests of unworthy outsiders.

But his great speech, and one of the best and greatest that he ever made, was the one in opposition to the Kansas-Nebraska bill, which was being pushed through Congress by the fire-eaters and their Northern pro-slavery followers. His own position upon the measure was best expressed by the words he used in commenting on the remarks of a Georgian member: "He votes as a Southern man, and votes sectionally; I also am a Southern man, but vote nationally on national questions."

The Missouri Compromise of 1820 had expressly abolished slavery in the territory out of which Kansas and Nebraska were carved. By the proposed bill this compromise was to be repealed, and the famous doctrine of non-intervention, or "squatter sovereignty," was to take its place, the people of each territory being allowed to choose for themselves whether they did or did not wish slavery. Benton attacked the proposal with all the strength of his frank, open nature as "a bungling attempt to smuggle slavery into the territory, and throughout all the country, up to the Canada line and out to the Rocky Mountains." He showed exhaustively the real nature of the original Missouri Compromise, which, as he said, was forced by the South upon the North, and which the South now proposed to repeal, that it might humiliate the North still further. The compromise of 1820 was, he justly contended, right; it was like the original compromises of the Constitution, by which the Slave States were admitted to the formation of the Union; no greater concession of principle was involved in the one case than in the other; and, had either compromise failed, the Union would not now be in existence. But the day when compromises had been necessary, or even harmless, had passed. The time had come when the extension of slavery was to be opposed in every constitutional way; and it was an outrage to propose to extend its domain by repealing all that part of a compromise measure which worked against it, when the South had already long taken advantage of such parts of the law as worked in its favor. Said Benton: "The South divided and took half, and now it will not do to claim the other half." Exactly as a proposition to destroy the slavery compromises of the Constitution would be an open attempt to destroy the Union, so, he said, the attempt to abrogate the compromise of 1820 would be a preparation for the same ending. "I have stood upon the Missouri Compromise for about thirty years, and mean to stand upon it to the end of my life ... [it is] a binding covenant upon both parties, and the more so upon the South, as she imposed it."

The squatter sovereignty theories of Douglas he treated with deserved ridicule, laughing at the idea that the territories were not the actual property of the nation, to be treated as the latter wished, and having none of the rights of sovereign states; and he condemned even more severely the theory advanced to the effect that Congress had no power to legislate on slavery in the territories. Thus, he pointed out that to admit any such theories was directly to reverse the principles upon which we had acted for seventy years in regard to the various territories that from time to time grew to such size as entitled them to come into the Union as states. After showing that there was no excuse for bringing in the bill on the plea of settling the slavery question, since there was not a foot of territory in the United States where the subject of slavery was not already settled by law, he closed with an earnest appeal against such an attempt to break up the Union and outrage the North by forcing slavery into a land where its existence was already forbidden by law. His speech exceeded the hour allotted to it, and he was allowed to go on only by the courtesy of a member from Illinois, who, when some of the Southerners protested against his being heard farther, gave up part of his own time to the grand old Missourian, and asked the House to hear him, if only "as the oldest living man in Congress, the only man in Congress who was present at the passage of the Missouri Compromise bill." Many a man at the North, ashamed and indignant at seeing the politicians of his own section cower at the crack of the Southern whip, felt a glow of sincere gratitude and admiration for the rugged Westerner, who so boldly bade defiance to the ruling slave party that held the reins not only in his own section, but also in his own state, and to oppose which was almost certain political death.

The Gadsden treaty was also strongly opposed and condemned by Benton, who considered it to be part of a great scheme or movement in the interests of the slavery disunionists, of which he also believed the Kansas-Nebraska bill to be the first development,—the "thin end of the wedge." He opposed the acquirement even of the small piece of territory we were actually able to purchase from Mexico; and showed good grounds for his belief that the administration, acting as usual only in the interest of the secessionists, had tried to get enough North-Mexican territory to form several new states, and had also attempted to purchase Cuba, both efforts being for the purpose of enabling the South either to become again dominant in the Union or else to set up a separate confederacy of her own. For it must be kept in mind that Benton always believed that the Southern disunion movements were largely due to conspiracies among ambitious politicians, who used the slavery question as a handle by which to influence the mass of the people. This view has certainly more truth in it than it is now the fashion to admit. His objection to the actual treaty was mainly based on its having been done by the executive without the consent of the legislature, and he also criticised it for the secrecy with which it had been put through. In bringing forward the first objection, however, he was confronted with Jefferson's conduct in acquiring Louisiana, which he endeavored, not very successfully, to show had nothing in common with the actions of Pierce, who, he said, simply demanded a check from the House with which to complete a purchase undertaken on his own responsibility.

Throughout his congressional term of service, Benton acted so as to deserve well of the Union as a whole, and most well of Missouri in particular. But he could not stem the tide of folly and madness in this state, and was defeated when he was a candidate for reëlection. The Whigs had now disappeared from the political arena, and the Know-nothings were running through their short and crooked lease of life; they foolishly nominated a third candidate in Benton's district, who drew off enough votes from him to enable his pro-slavery Democratic competitor to win.

No sooner had he lost his seat in Congress than Benton, indefatigable as ever, set to work to finish his "Thirty Years' View," and produced the second volume in 1856, the year when he made his last attempt to regain his hold in politics, and to win Missouri back to the old Union standard. Although his own son-in-law, Fremont, the daring western explorer, was running as the first presidential candidate ever nominated by the Republicans, the old partisan voted for the Democrat, Buchanan. He did not like Buchanan, considering him weak and unsuitable, but the Republican party he believed to be entirely too sectional in character for him to give it his support. For governor there was a triangular fight, the Know-nothings having nominated one candidate, the secessionist Democrats a second, while Benton himself ran as the choice of the Union Democracy. He was now seventy-four years old, but his mind was as vigorous as ever, and his iron will kept up a frame that had hardly even yet begun to give way. During the course of the campaign he traveled throughout the state, going in all twelve hundred miles, and making forty speeches, each one of two or three hours' length. This was a remarkable feat for so old a man; indeed, it has very rarely been paralleled, except by Gladstone's recent performances. The vote was quite evenly divided between the three candidates; but Benton came in third, and the extreme pro-slavery men carried the day. After this, during the few months of life he yet had left, he did not again mingle in the politics of Missouri.

But in the days of his defeat at home, the regard and respect in which he was held in the other states, especially at the North, increased steadily; and in the fall of 1856 he made by request a lecturing tour in New England, speaking on the danger of the political situation and the imperative necessity of preserving the Union, which he now clearly saw to be gravely threatened. He was well received, for the North was learning to respect him, and he had gotten over his early hostility to New England,—a hostility originally shared by the whole West. The New Englanders were not yet aware, however, of the importance of the secession movements, and paid little heed to the warnings that were to be so fully justified by the events of the next few years. But Benton, in spite of his great age, saw distinctly the changes that were taking place, and the dangers that were impending,—an unusual thing for a man whose active life has already been lived out under widely different conditions.

He again turned his attention to literature, and produced another great work, the "Abridgment of the Debates of Congress from 1787 to 1856," in sixteen volumes, besides writing a valuable pamphlet on the Dred Scott decision, which he severely criticised. The amount of labor all this required was immense, and his health completely gave way; yet he continued working to the very end, dictating the closing portion of the "Abridgment" in a whisper as he lay on his death-bed. When he once began to fail his advanced years made him succumb rapidly; and on April 10, 1858, he died, in the city of Washington. As soon as the news reached Missouri, a great revulsion of feeling took place, and all classes of the people united to do honor to the memory of the dead statesman, realizing that they had lost a man who towered head and shoulders above both friends and foes. The body was taken to St. Louis, and after lying in state was buried in Bellefontaine Cemetery, more than forty thousand people witnessing the funeral. All the public buildings were draped in mourning; all places of business were closed, and the flags everywhere were at half-mast. Thus at the very end the great city of the West at last again paid fit homage to the West's mightiest son.

Benton's most important writings are those mentioned above. The "Thirty Years' View" ("a history of the working of the American government for thirty years, from 1820 to 1850") will always be indispensable to every student of American history. It deals with the deeds of both houses of Congress, and of some of the higher federal officials during his thirty years' term of service in the Senate, and is valuable alike for the original data it contains, and because it is so complete a record of our public life at that time. The book is also remarkable for its courteous and equable tone, even towards bitter personal and political enemies. It shows a vanity on the part of the author that is too frank and free from malice to be anything but amusing; the style is rather ponderous, and the English not always good, for Benton began life, and, in fact, largely passed it, in an age of ornate periods, when grandiloquence was considered more essential than grammar. In much of the Mississippi valley the people had their own canons of literary taste; indeed, in a recent book by one of Benton's admirers, there is a fond allusion to his statement, anent the expunging resolution, that "solitary and alone" he had set the ball in motion,—the pleonasm being evidently looked upon in the light of a rather fine oratorical outburst.

"The Abridgment of the Debates of Congress from 1789 to 1856" he was only able to bring down to 1850. Sixteen volumes were published. It was a compilation needing infinite labor, and is invaluable to the historian. While in the midst of the vast work he also found time to write his "Examination of the Dred Scott case," in so far as it decided the Missouri Compromise law to be unconstitutional, and asserted the self-extension of the Constitution into the territories, carrying slavery with it,—the decision in this case promulgated by Judge Taney, of unhappy fame, having been the last step taken in the interests of slavery and for the overthrow of freedom. The pamphlet contained nearly two hundred pages, and showed, as was invariably the case with anything Benton did, the effects of laborious research and wide historical and legal learning. His summing up was, "that the decision conflicts with the uniform action of all the departments of the federal government from its foundation to the present time, and cannot be accepted as a rule to govern Congress and the people, without severing that act and admitting the political supremacy of the court and accepting an altered constitution from its hands, and taking a new and portentous point of departure in the working of the government." He denounced the new party theories of the Democracy, which had abandoned the old belief of the founders of the Republic, that Congress had power to legislate upon slavery in territories, and which had gone on "from the abrogation of the Missouri Compromise, which saved the Union, to squatter sovereignty, which killed the compromise, and thence to the decisions of the supreme court, which kill both." In closing he touched briefly on the history of the pro-slavery agitation. "Up to Mr. Pierce's administration the plan had been defensive, that is to say, to make the secession of the South a measure of self-defense against the abolition encroachments and crusades of the North. In the time of Mr. Pierce the plan became offensive, that is to say, to commence the expansion of slavery, and the acquisition of territory to spread it over, so as to overpower the North with new Slave States, and drive them out of the Union.... The rising in the Free States, in consequence of the abrogation of the Missouri Compromise, checked these schemes, and limited the success of the disunionists to the revival of the agitation which enables them to wield the South against the North in all the federal elections and all federal legislation. Accidents and events have given the party a strange preëminence,—under Jackson's administration proclaimed for treason; since at the head of the government and of the Democratic party. The death of Harrison, and the accession of Tyler, was their first great lift; the election of Mr. Pierce was their culminating point." This was the last protest of the last of the old Jacksonian leaders against that new generation of Democrats, whose delight it had become to bow down to strange gods.

In his private life Benton's relations were of the pleasantest. He was a religious man, although, like his great political chief, he could on occasions swear roundly. He was rigidly moral, and he was too fond of work ever to make social life a business. But he liked small dinners, with just a few intimate friends or noted and brilliant public men, and always shone at such an entertainment. Although he had not traveled much, he gave the impression of having done so, by reason of his wide reading, and because he always made a point of knowing all explorers, especially those who had penetrated our great western wilds. His geographical knowledge was wonderful; and his good nature, as well as his delight in work for work's sake, made him of more use than any library of reference, if his friends needed information upon some abstruse matter,—Webster himself acknowledging his indebtedness to him on one occasion, and being the authority for the statement that Benton knew more political facts than any other man he had ever met, even than John Quincy Adams, and possessed a wonderful fund of general knowledge. Although very gentle in his dealings with those for whom he cared, Benton originally was rather quarrelsome and revengeful in character. His personal and political prejudices were bitter, and he denounced his enemies freely in public and from the stump; yet he always declined to take part in joint political debates, on account of the personal discourtesy with which they were usually conducted. He gave his whole time to public life, rarely or never attending to his law practice after he had fairly entered the political field.

Benton was one of those who were present and escaped death at the time of the terrible accident on board the Princeton, during Tyler's administration, when the bursting of her great gun killed so many prominent men. Benton was saved owing to the fact that, characteristically enough, he had stepped to one side the better to note the marksmanship of the gunner. Ex-Governor Gilmer, of Virginia, who had taken his place, was instantly killed. Tyler, who was also on board, was likewise saved in consequence of the exhibition of a characteristic trait; for, just as the gun was about to be fired, something occurred in another part of the ship which distracted the attention of the fussy, fidgety president, who accordingly ran off to see what it was, and thus escaped the fatal explosion. The tragic nature of the accident and his own narrow escape made a deep impression upon Benton; and it was noticed that ever afterwards he was far more forbearing and forgiving than of old. He became good friends with Webster and other political opponents, with whom he had formerly hardly been on speaking terms. Calhoun alone he would never forgive. It was not in his nature to do anything by halves; and accordingly, when he once forgave an opponent, he could not do enough to show him that the forgiveness was real. A Missourian named Wilson, who had been his bitter and malignant political foe for years, finally becoming broken in fortune and desirous of bettering himself by going to California, where Benton's influence, through his son-in-law, Fremont, was supreme, was persuaded by Webster to throw himself on the generosity of his old enemy. The latter not only met him half-way, but helped him with a lavish kindness that would hardly have been warranted by less than a life-long friendship. Webster has left on record the fact that, when once they had come to be on good terms with each other, there was no man in the whole Senate of whom he would more freely have asked any favor that could properly be granted.

He was a most loving father. At his death he left four surviving daughters,— Mrs. William Carey Jones, Mrs. Sarah Benton Jacobs, Madame Susan Benton Boilleau, and Mrs. Jessie Ann Benton Fremont, the wife of the great explorer, whose wonderful feats and adventures, ending with the conquest of California, where he became a sort of viceroy in point of power, made him an especial favorite with his father-in-law, who loved daring and hardihood. Benton took the keenest delight in Fremont's remarkable successes, and was never tired of talking of them, both within and without the Senate. He records with very natural pride the fact that it was only the courage and judgment displayed in a trying crisis by his own gifted daughter, Fremont's wife, which enabled the adventurous young explorer to prosecute one of the most important of his expeditions, when threatened with fatal interference from jealous governmental superiors.

He was an exceptionally devoted husband. His wife was Miss Elizabeth McDowell, of Virginia, whom he married after he had entered the Senate. Their life was most happy until 1844, when she was struck by paralysis. From that time till her death in 1854, he never went out to a public place of amusement, spending all his time not occupied with public duties in writing by her bedside. It is scant praise to say that, while mere acquiescence on his part would have enabled him to become rich through government influence, he nevertheless died a poor man. In public, as in private life, he was a man of sensitive purity of character; he would never permit any person connected with him by blood or marriage to accept office under the government, nor would he ever favor any applicant for a government contract on political grounds.

During his last years, when his sturdy independence and devotion to the Union had caused him the loss of his political influence in his own state and with his own party, he nevertheless stood higher with the country at large than ever before. He was a faithful friend and a bitter foe; he was vain, proud, utterly fearless, and quite unable to comprehend such emotions as are expressed by the terms despondency and yielding. Without being a great orator or writer, or even an original thinker, he yet possessed marked ability; and his abounding vitality and marvelous memory, his indomitable energy and industry, and his tenacious persistency and personal courage, all combined to give him a position and influence such as few American statesmen have ever held. His character grew steadily to the very last; he made better speeches and was better able to face new problems when past three score and ten than in his early youth or middle age. He possessed a rich fund of political, legal, and historical learning, and every subject that he ever handled showed the traces of careful and thorough study. He was very courteous, except when provoked; his courage was proof against all fear, and he shrank from no contest, personal or political. He was sometimes narrow-minded, and always wilful and passionate; but he was honest and truthful. At all times and in all places he held every good gift he had completely at the service of the American Federal Union.

FOOTNOTES

[1] Justin McCarthy.

[2] Aurelian.

Milton Keynes UK
Ingram Content Group UK Ltd.
UKHW031047120324
439302UK00006B/517